THE
MIRACLE
OF
RICHFIELD

The MIRACLE *of* RICHFIELD

The Story of the 1975–76 Cleveland Cavaliers

Roger Gordon
Foreword by
Nate Thurmond

Black Squirrel Books™
Kent, Ohio

Black Squirrel Books™ 🐿️ ™
Frisky, industrious black squirrels are a familiar sight on the Kent State University campus and the inspiration for Black Squirrel Books™, a trade imprint of The Kent State University Press. www.KentStateUniversityPress.com.

Library of Congress Catalog Number 2016007533
ISBN 978-1-60635-277-9

Library of Congress Cataloging-in-Publication Data
Names: Gordon, Roger, author.
Title: The miracle of Richfield : the story of the 1975-76 Cleveland Cavaliers / Roger Gordon ; foreword by Nate Thurmond.
Description: Kent, Ohio : Kent State University, [2016] | Includes bibliographical references and index.
Identifiers: LCCN 2016007533 (print) | LCCN 2016014906 (ebook) | ISBN 9781606352779 (pbk. : alk. paper) | ISBN 9781631012488 (ePub) | ISBN 9781631012495 (ePDF)
Subjects: LCSH: Cleveland Cavaliers (Basketball team)--History.
Classification: LCC GV885.52.C57 G67 2016 (print) | LCC GV885.52.C57 (ebook) | DDC 796.323/640977132--dc23
LC record available at http://lccn.loc.gov/2016007533

20 19 18 17 16   5 4 3 2 1

Contents

The Wine and Gold

Foreword

Nate Thurmond,
Center, Cleveland Cavaliers,
1975–77

It's hard to believe, but it's been more than 40 years since I returned home and joined the Cavaliers. It was Thanksgiving Day 1975. I was in my second season with the Chicago Bulls after 11, if I may say, successful years with the Warriors. Long past my prime, I was the Bulls' backup center. I'd have a good game every now and then, but it was painfully obvious that I simply didn't fit in their plans. When I received word that I'd been traded to the Cavaliers, I was thrilled. Not only was I leaving a lousy situation in Chicago, I was coming home! I was born and raised in Akron. It was wonderful coming back to Northeast Ohio. My family and friends were there, and they all could come see me play since The Coliseum was just a stone's throw from the "Rubber City."

I was brought to Cleveland mainly to spell talented starting center Jim Chones for 15 or so minutes per game. The Cavs had not been playing very well. They'd lost 10 of their first 16 games. I thought the team had some talent, though. They had different guys who could score, but they needed a little bit of defensive toughness. That's where I came in. No, I wasn't exactly Wilt Chamberlain offensively, but who was? I could still put the ball in the hoop. Defense, though, is what I staked my reputation on. Blocking shots was my paradise, what I lived for.

I thrived in my role of backing up Jim. My hard work on defense began to rub off on him and the other players. We soon reeled off seven straight wins. Before we knew it, we were in a season-long battle with the Washington Bullets for the top spot in the Central Division. We clinched a playoff spot. We won the division.

The utter excitement surrounding our playoff series with the Bullets will live with me forever. Those fans at The Coliseum were absolutely mad! I'd never been involved in anything like that before and haven't since. With crowds like that, if I'd been there five years earlier when I was dealing, when I was at the height of my career, there's no telling what I could've done. Those unbelievable fans were my motivation. When I heard the crowd roaring before the games, it sent chills up and down my spine. In the locker room, we could hear the fans stomping on the cement. I've got tears in my eyes right now just writing about it. It was like having a sixth man with you. Nothing was going to deter you from your job. Those people had you on your p's and q's. You wanted to do everything right with the crowd behind you. That's what it did for me.

It was certainly disappointing when Jim broke his right foot a couple of days before our Eastern Conference Championship Series with the Boston Celtics. Had he not gotten hurt, I believe we would've beaten Boston and gone on to win the NBA title. I gave it all I had in those six games with the Celtics. We nearly forced a seventh game, and who knows? Anything can happen in a Game 7.

I played in two NBA Finals with the Warriors. The Miracle of Richfield, though, does not take a backseat to anything I experienced in my career, including those two Finals appearances. I'm not saying the Miracle of Richfield was more important than getting to the Finals, but the aura around it seemed greater. And the number of people pulling for us was far and above those other two situations. We may not have won the NBA Championship, or even played in the Finals, that season, but the 1975–76 Cleveland Cavaliers and their fans developed a bond that gave new meaning to the word special.

Preface

I was fast asleep when Dick Snyder banked in the winning basket in Game 7 against Washington. On that Thursday evening, April 29, 1976, when Phil Chenier missed a jumper from the right corner a few moments later to end the game, I was still snoozing, according to my older brother Bruce, who, like hundreds of thousands of Cavaliers fans, was tuned into WWWE-AM 1100—3WE to Cavs fans back then—listening to Joe Tait's every word as he called the action (astonishingly, the game was not televised in the Cleveland area).

When Tait described the then-NBA record playoff crowd of 21,564 going berserk, while many rushed The Coliseum floor to celebrate the Cavs' remarkable, thrilling victory over the favored, playoff-tested Bullets to give them a 4–3 series victory, I was probably dreaming about Kirsten, a cute little blonde in my third-grade class whom I wanted to marry. Bruce, meanwhile, was going crazy, jubilant that the Cavaliers were on their way to face the mighty, but beatable, Boston Celtics for the Eastern Conference Championship, a series the Cavs would lose in six tough games.

As it turned out, I missed experiencing the Miracle of Richfield by about a month. My interest in the NBA, and professional sports in general, was born some five weeks later on June 4 when I saw on television the classic Phoenix-Boston triple-overtime thriller—considered by many to be the greatest NBA game ever played—in Game 5 of the Finals. It was the very first sporting event I remember watching on the tube. And by the time the 1976–77 season arrived the next October, I was a full-fledged Cavs fan—for life.

Acknowledgments

I would like to thank Joyce Harrison of The Kent State University Press for allowing me the opportunity to write this book, and everyone else there, especially managing editor Mary Young, for their assistance. I would also like to thank the many people I interviewed, especially Bill Fitch and Mike Peticca. Gratitude also goes out to The Cleveland Press Collection in the Michael Schwartz Library at Cleveland State University and Andersons-ClevelandDesign.com for providing photos.

Special thanks to the late Nate Thurmond for penning the foreword.

BEGINNINGS

1 | B.C. (Before the Cavs)

It's ironic. When the finest professional basketball players in the world represented Cleveland, Ohio, nearly a century ago, the team folded in just its sixth season. But when the same town fielded some of the world's *worst* pros some 45 years later, that team not only stuck it out but is alive and well today. The 1970–71 expansion Cleveland Cavaliers lost their first 15 games and finished with an embarrassing 15–67 record, a .183 winning percentage, one of the worst seasons in National Basketball Association history. Despite the Cavs' horrible early years and some terrible times since then, the team today plays before sellouts at every home game and is on the rise once again after some recent tumultuous seasons.

Whereas the Cavaliers struggled early on but survived, the Cleveland Rosenblums of the American Basketball League succeeded from the start but called it quits soon after. The Rosenblums won three ABL championships in the late 1920s but went out of business toward the end of 1930, after just five-and-a-half seasons as Cleveland's first pro basketball team. The Rosenblums' quick rise and fall was a sign of things to come for professional basketball in Cleveland during the following four decades when the popularity of pro hoops was not even close to what it eventually would become.

The Rosenblums, also known as the "Rosies," actually were formed long before the ABL, the first major professional basketball league in the United States, was created in 1925. The team was organized some 15 years earlier by founder and owner Max Rosenblum, a Cleveland department store owner, as a pro team that played its home games at Public Hall but also barnstormed around the country.

The Cleveland Arena circa 1950. (Courtesy of AndersonsClevelandDesign.com)

The 1919 Rosenblums compiled an 18–2 record and were chosen by Cleveland sports editors as "the recognized champions of Ohio." Six years later the ABL was established, and the Rosies won three of the first five league championships. The Great Depression was causing fewer and fewer fans to show up around the league, and Cleveland was no exception. Rosenblum shocked the basketball world when, on December 8, 1930, he announced a dozen games into the season that his team would cease operations due to poor attendance. The ABL itself was in such financial straits that it suspended operations for the next two seasons. It was reorganized in 1933–34 but was no longer "big league," especially with the birth of the National Basketball League in 1937. The reborn ABL never really took off and ultimately folded in the mid-1950s.

The NBL was mainly made up of Great Lakes–area small-market and corporate teams. Some were independent, while others were owned by companies that also found jobs for their players. Cleveland's first entry in the NBL was the White Horses, who relocated from Warren, where they were known as the Penns, on February 10, 1939, about two-thirds of the way into the schedule. The team folded after the season. Five years later the league persuaded the Chase Brass Company, a large manufacturing business in Euclid, to sponsor a team. The result was Cleveland's second entry in the NBL—the Chase Brassmen, who were led by pivot man Mel Riebe. Riebe led the NBL in scoring with 17.9 points per game and won the league's Rookie of the Year honor.

"Riebe never met a shot he didn't like. He knew how to score," said in 2005 the late Bill Nichols, the Cavaliers' beat writer for the *Plain Dealer* during the Miracle of Richfield season, who had seen Riebe play years earlier.

"I wrote a couple of columns years and years ago," former *Plain Dealer* sportswriter Bob Dolgan said, "to the effect that Mel Riebe was the greatest basketball player that Cleveland ever produced until the time Clark Kellogg emerged. Riebe was a husky guy but also very fast and quick who played with his back to the basket."

Despite Riebe's marvelous play, the Chase Brassmen, who played some of their home games at Riebe's alma mater, Euclid Shore High School, won just three of 18 games and lost in the first round of the playoffs (each of the NBL's four teams qualified for the postseason). The next year the Cleveland team changed sponsors and was known as the Allmen Transfers. That team was an improvement but still won just 13 of 30 games before falling to an appalling 4–29 in 1945–46. The club folded after the season.

That summer owners of some of the country's biggest sports arenas, led by Madison Square Garden's Ned Irish, the Boston Garden's Walter Brown, and the downtown Cleveland Arena's Al Sutphin, decided the time was right to bring major league professional basketball to the largest cities. With World War II over, many more players were available. And the lifting of wartime restrictions on the economy allowed Americans more money to spend on entertainment. On June 6, 1946, the Basketball Association of America was created in New York City. Because the BAA was in direct competition with the NBL for the best graduating college players, the new outfit wanted offense and a lot of it; thus all varieties of zone defense were prohibited. Man-to-man was the only defense allowed.

Cleveland was awarded one of the 11 teams—the Rebels. Other teams included the Boston Celtics, New York Knickerbockers, and Philadelphia Warriors. The Rebels played their home games at the nine-year-old Cleveland Arena. Led by Riebe, they finished 30–30 in 1946–47 and lost in the first round of the playoffs. They folded after the season.

"It just wasn't time yet for pro basketball to make it in Cleveland," Nichols said.

The BAA lasted two more seasons. Then, in 1949, it agreed to absorb several teams from the NBL, which dissolved after the 1948–49 season, creating what was then a 17-team National Basketball Association. The NBA grew in stature as the years went on, through the 1950s and into the early '60s. The

Minneapolis (now Los Angeles) Lakers were the gem of the NBA from the start. Led by 6-foot-10, 245-pound giant George Mikan, the Lakers, one of the NBL teams that was absorbed into the NBA, won four of the first five NBA Championships after having won the last BAA title in 1949. Three years after the Lakers' run ended, the Celtics began a string of titles that would become one of the greatest dynasties in sports history. Led by center Bill Russell and a cast of greats, Boston would win 11 championships in 13 seasons from 1956–57 through 1968–69.

Almost right smack in the middle of the Celtics' historic run, pro basketball returned to Cleveland once again in 1961 with George Streinbrenner's Pipers of the new eight-team ABL. Steinbrenner, a Bay Village native and future owner of the New York Yankees, bought the team from a plumbing-business owner named Ed Sweeny, hence the name "Pipers." The Pipers had enjoyed great success for years as a Cleveland industrial team. Led by Dick Barnett, who had spent two solid seasons with the NBA's Syracuse Nationals, and future NBAers Johnny Cox and Ben Warley, the Pipers, who played most of their home games at Public Hall, won the 1961–62 ABL championship.

"We covered the Pipers at *The Plain Dealer* on a regular basis," recalled in 2005 the late Hal Lebovitz, a Cleveland sportswriting legend who began at the *Cleveland News* in 1946 and later was sports editor of the *Plain Dealer* for nearly 20 years. "They did well and were always making news, but the city was just not excited about them."

"It was a Browns and Indians town," said Nichols.

After signing former Ohio State and soon-to-be Cincinnati Royals star Jerry Lucas, Steinbrenner was unable to convince the NBA to accept his team, and the Pipers folded before Lucas played even one game for them. The ABL itself was unable to compete with the NBA and went out of business on December 31, 1962, during its second season.

The Pipers may have been history, but there was still professional basketball to be played in Cleveland before the 1960s were through. As the Celtics' dominance of the NBA continued, the league was growing and building a niche for itself in the sports fandom across the country. Besides Russell and other Boston greats like John Havlicek, Bob Cousy, and Tom Heinsohn, there were other stars around the NBA such as Wilt "The Stilt" Chamberlain, Elgin Baylor, Oscar Robertson, and Lucas. Beginning in 1966, many of these players paid visits to Cleveland now and then, some—Robertson and Lucas—more than others.

The Cleveland Pipers' Ben Warley (32) and Johnny Cox (24) in action against the Hawaii Chiefs. (The Cleveland Press Collection, Michael Schwartz Library, Cleveland State University)

"While I was sports editor of *The Plain Dealer*," Lebovitz recalled, "I always tried to come up with promotions for the paper that would increase our circulation and raise money for charity. We had Bat Day, Ball Day, and Grandstand Manager Night for the Indians. So I went to Nate Wallick, the vice president of public relations for the Browns, and told him I'd like to bring in the NBA's Cincinnati Royals—who had Robertson and Lucas—to Cleveland for 10 games per season."

"The Royals were not drawing too well in Cincinnati," Dolgan said.

"I wanted to see if the Browns would sponsor the games in case we lost money," Lebovitz said. "And Wallick got Art Modell to say yes. So we talked to the guy who ran the Royals and made a deal with him, and then we made a deal with the Cleveland Arena. It was an unbelievable deal— $10,000 a game for 10 games! *The Plain Dealer* paid the Royals, but it was underwritten by Modell. We didn't have to pay the referees or anything. All we had to do was pay for the rental of the Arena and the $10,000 per game. All the money after the Royals were paid—the profits—went to Plain

Dealer Charities. All the NBA stars and the great teams would come to town and play. We packed 'em in, too, and made a lot of money! The next year I wanted the Royals back. They raised the price to $15,000 a game and I grabbed it. Modell underwrote it again."

"Everyone in Cleveland called the team the Ohio Royals," Dolgan laughed.

The Royals continued to call Cleveland their home 10 times a season through 1969–70.

"We were so successful with the Royals," Lebovitz said, "that Walter Kennedy, the NBA commissioner at the time, wanted to put a franchise in Cleveland. He and I became good friends. He told me right around 1968 to get some Clevelanders together and come to New York for a meeting with a $50,000, maybe a $100,000, down payment. That's all we needed! It's hard to believe!"

So Lebovitz went to work—and fast—rounding up an impressive array of men that included Ted Bonda, who later would become owner and president of the Indians; Howard Metzenbaum, a local politician who eventually would serve nearly 20 years as a U.S. senator; and Armand Aronson, a well-known publisher and author.

"We all met up on the 10th floor of the Union Bank of Commerce Building on East Ninth and Euclid," Lebovitz recalled. "I also had George Herzog, president of the bank, there. We came up with the money, that was no problem. And, as I recall, Howard had to go to New York anyway. So Howard took the money and left for New York to meet with the NBA guys. Now, these were a bunch of guys who were very independent, *very* independent. They didn't give a damn about anything. They were holding their meeting at some hotel, and Howard was sitting outside the room, and he sat . . . and he sat . . . and he sat. They didn't call him in, he got mad, and he came back home with the money. He was insulted. You don't take a man like Howard Metzenbaum and let him sit for five, six hours without even coming out and saying hello. I called Walter and I said, 'What happened?' He said, 'Howard disappeared.' And I said, 'Hell, why didn't you call me? At least I could've put in a call to him!' So we didn't get the franchise.

"Then Nick Mileti came along."

And by the time a new decade would dawn, pro basketball would be back in town—but this time for the long haul.

2 | Nick Mileti's Early Years

He felt it was time. It was as simple as that. Nick Mileti believed Cleveland was in dire need of an NBA franchise.

"The Cavaliers were founded because they needed to be founded," Mileti, a Cleveland native, said on the record album *Miracle in Richfield—The Cavalier Happening.* "We had a situation when we bought the (Cleveland) Arena and the Barons in 1968 where we had Cleveland, Ohio, the eighth-(largest) market in the United States of America, with no professional basketball . . . no professional basketball! Towns like Milwaukee, towns like Seattle, towns like Phoenix . . . nice people live there and they're nice towns, but they're *small* towns and *they* had NBA basketball, and here we were in our town without it."

Mileti traveled a long road on his way to founding Cleveland's first-ever NBA team. He was born on April 22, 1931, and was raised in a working-class neighborhood in the southeast end of town. He attended John Adams High School, from which he graduated in 1949. Putting to use an arduous work ethic, a business savvy that included numerous contacts, and a high energy level, Mileti put himself through college and graduated from Bowling Green State University in 1953. Bowling Green's Mileti Alumni Center is named in his honor. Mileti then earned a law degree from Ohio State University. After serving in the military, he opened a law practice in Lakewood and became prosecutor there. He also served as chairman of the Bowling Green Alumni Association.

"Nobody had ever heard of Mileti, nobody knew who he was," said Bob Dolgan. "He just showed up and bought the Barons and the Arena."

Not only did Mileti believe that Cleveland needed an NBA team, he also felt the Arena needed another tenant. He organized an ownership group and went to work immediately.

"One of the first calls I made was to Walter Kennedy," he said. "We started a series of negotiations that took from the end of '68 until we put the team together and got the franchise in April of '70."

"Nick was a hustler guy, very aggressive," Bill Nichols said. "He was a manipulator but in a positive sense. He could put packages of people together to buy teams."

"Nick didn't have a lot of money but he had investors," added Sheldon Ocker, the Cavaliers' beat writer for the *Akron Beacon Journal* from 1971–81. "And even so, I think it was mostly on kind of a shoestring deal. Nick was a salesman, a good salesman. He was the kind of guy who could talk you into loaning him a million dollars on Monday, he'd blow it on Wednesday, and the following Monday you'd loan him another million. He just had that kind of personality, kind of a magnetic personality. He was real outgoing, a very likeable guy. He was certainly good for us, the media, to deal with."

Mileti's group paid $3.7 million for the expansion team that, with the help of a name-the-team contest in the *Plain Dealer* that drew more than 14,000 entries, would be called the Cavaliers; Mileti made the final call. The team colors of wine and gold emanated from the hues of Mileti's high school alma mater. The wine was changed to a "Cavaliers wine" to set the team apart somewhat. The jerseys featured a feathered treatment of the letter "C" in "Cavaliers." The primary color on the home uniform was gold and on the road uniform was wine. The team logo was that of a swashbuckling cavalier with a pointing sword looking left, surrounded by the team name and a basketball. The old, run-down Arena, with a seating capacity of less than 10,000, would be the team's home.

Ocker recalled fan reaction to the news that the Cavaliers were coming into existence as less than vigorous.

"It wasn't as big a deal as it would be now," he said. "It was like, 'Hey, we've got an NBA franchise, that's nice. Now, let's try to get an NHL team.'"

Even though the town was not exactly rolling out the red carpet for the Cavs, Cleveland finally had an NBA team. It would begin play in the fall of 1970.

The next step? Finding a head coach.

3 | Bill Fitch

"Hello?"

It was Nick Mileti on the other end of the line. It was 5:00 A.M. "He wanted me to be the head coach of the Cleveland Cavaliers," Bill Fitch said. It was March 1970, and Fitch was the 38-year-old head coach at the University of Minnesota. One would think that, after 14 years—and five schools—of working his way up the college coaching ladder, Fitch would have jumped at the opportunity to become a head coach in the NBA. He didn't, though. At least not immediately.

"I'd already achieved my ultimate goal," he said. "I wanted to coach in the Big Ten. I was from that area. I wanted to coach at either Minnesota or Iowa, whichever one wanted me first." So when he received a phone call from Minnesota athletic director Marsh Ryman in 1968 offering him the Golden Gophers' head coaching job, Fitch, the head coach at Bowling Green State University at the time, couldn't resist.

"When I was hired at Bowling Green a year earlier," he said, "I made a commitment to Doyt Perry, the AD there, that I'd stay there as long as he wanted me. I told him to forget about a contract—unless Iowa or Minnesota came after me." And a year later Minnesota came calling. Fitch led the Gophers to a 12–12 record in 1968–69 and a 13–11 record in 1969–70. Those marks were not outstanding, but considering the team had won just 16 games combined the two previous seasons, they were reason to celebrate.

"We'd built a good team at Minnesota, including Jim Brewer, a future player of mine on the Cavs," Fitch said, "that was ready to contend for a Big Ten title the next season."

Fitch was happy. He was where he wanted to be . . . at least he thought so. His long road to the Twin Cities began when he was born on May 19, 1932, in Davenport, Iowa. He was raised in Cedar Rapids and gained an interest in athletics at an early age.

"When I was 8," he said, "I lied and said I was 9 so I could play in a baseball league. Baseball was my first sport but I ended up playing them all."

While attending Wilson High School Fitch played quarterback on the football team, guard on the basketball team, was a member of the track and field team, and was the catcher on the baseball team that won two state championships.

"I don't know if I was worth a damn in any of 'em," he laughed. "I was just lucky enough to play." He was a terrific basketball player, though, and was offered a full scholarship to play for living legend Phog Allen at the University of Kansas.

"My mom and dad wanted me to go there," he said, "and that's where I was going to go. Allen could recruit the cat and the dog and take mom and dad with him. He was a good salesman. But then he sent a letter to all of his out-of-state recruits—including myself—to let us know that they weren't able to get us in. Being out-of-state students, we weren't protected from the draft because we couldn't get into the ROTC program. It was all filled up with in-state students."

So Fitch stayed in Cedar Rapids and attended Coe College, with its ROTC program, on a full ride for basketball. "It was the only school I could spell at the time anyhow," the ever-amusing Fitch said.

Fitch was a key cog on a Coe team that enjoyed great success and was co-champion of the Midwest Conference his senior year. "I had a great experience at Coe," said Fitch, who majored in education and psychology. "When I graduated, I knew that coaching was what I wanted to do."

Fitch entered the service for two years before getting his first coaching gig in 1956 as an assistant at Creighton University, where he was also the head baseball coach. After two years at Creighton, Fitch returned to Coe as the head basketball and head baseball coach through 1962. He then went to the University of North Dakota as its head coach for five years and then to Bowling Green, where in 1967–68 he led the Falcons to an 18–7 record, the Mid-American Conference title, and the school's last appearance in the NCAA Tournament. Fitch was named Coach of the Year in Ohio.

"I would've stayed at Bowling Green forever," he said, "because it was a great school and I had a great time there. I'd recommend Bowling Green to any kid graduating from high school today."

After one year, though, Fitch was off to Minnesota. "Jim Lessig, a Bowling Green grad, had been my assistant coach at BG and I'd brought him to Minnesota my second year there," he said. "Jim and I had just driven from Iowa to Illinois and over to Hutchinson, Kansas, scouting the National Junior College tournament. And then I got that call from Nick in the wee hours of the morning. He'd come to our last two games that season to talk to me about the Cavs' coaching job."

Fitch said no the first time. He said no the second time. "I guess I didn't give him a *hard* enough no," he said, "but it wouldn't have made any difference because once Nick makes up his mind, it happens . . . he's just that type of guy. He could sell you the Brooklyn Bridge. And if he couldn't, he'd stay on you like a bulldog until he could."

The city of Cleveland, oddly enough, was a major factor in the onset of Fitch and Mileti's relationship. "Three years earlier I'd just taken the Bowling Green job," Fitch recalled, "and Nick wanted to convince everybody in Cleveland that he could turn it into a big-time basketball town. Bowling Green was scheduled to host Niagara when they had Calvin Murphy and Manny Leaks—big-time players—and he wanted Bowling Green to come over and play Niagara at the Cleveland Arena."

"Nick was a great promoter. He was such a wheeler-dealer," Hal Lebovitz said. "Bowling Green was a very good team that year."

"This," said Fitch, "was my first [and only] year at Bowling Green and I said, 'Hell, that's a good home game! We've got a chance to beat those guys if we play them at home, but if we play them over in Cleveland it's like a home game for them!' Well, Nick won that battle, too. I finally said, 'Okay. Okay then, we'll come over.' So we played the game in Cleveland and sold the place out. We won, too."

"From that," Lebovitz said, "I think Nick got the idea to try to get an NBA franchise."

"And that's why he came after me for the Cleveland job," said Fitch. "So when he called me early that morning when I was in Kansas for the junior college tourney, we talked until . . . it must've been 7:30."

It was a phone call that would change Fitch's life. "I finally agreed to take the job," he said. "I told Nick, 'I'll leave here right now and go back to Minnesota and tell the school president, Malcolm Moos,'" he said. "Jim stayed in Kansas to cover the tournament for me. I talked to Mr. Moos, I talked to Marsh, and I told them what I was going to do before it ever got out. They understood."

At last, Nick Mileti had his man.

4 | He's No Joe Schmo

Joe Tait was a terrible athlete while growing up in Illinois. "I played 'em all and I was bad at 'em all," he admitted. "I didn't have the coordination." Born in Evanston, a Chicago suburb, on May 15, 1937, Tait was five years old when his family moved to its farm about 100 miles west of the "Windy City."

"My father," he said, "felt the Nazis or Japs might someday drop a bomb on Chicago so he moved us to the farm. I enjoyed growing up on a farm. By the time I was a teenager we lived in West Aurora, a suburb about 40 miles west of the city. I was on the first wrestling team West Aurora High School had, and I went 0–6 in the heavyweight division. I also threw the shot in track and field but not very well. I practiced hard but rarely played until I blew out my knee, and that ended a less-than-spectacular athletic career."

Tait went off to Monmouth College in Monmouth, Illinois. "I was on a 3–2 plan," he said, "with the University of Missouri School of Journalism whereby I'd get all of my prerequisites out of the way, and then transfer to Missouri for my last two years. I wanted to be a writer, but I never made it to Missouri because I got into radio at a couple of stations while at Monmouth. I took a job as a janitor at one called WRAM. It fit into my schedule so I'd go down and clean the station, working my way through school. From time to time, an on-air person would get sick or quit and I'd sub for them. Eventually, I wasn't subbing anymore and I was working there on a full-time basis, doing everything from program director to play-by-play, including for Monmouth College sporting events, to reading the news. The boss liked me because I was cheap—a dollar an hour. That was the minimum wage in those days."

Tait graduated from Monmouth in 1959 and then spent three years in the Army Security Agency. He did his basic training at Fort Leonard Woods, Missouri, before entering the Defense Language Institute in Monterey, California. He then went overseas and was stationed in Sinop, Turkey, for 13 months.

"We built a radio station over there," Tait said, "and pirated things out of the air like Reuters news, the Indianapolis 500, Major League Baseball, football . . . we stole anything we could find up there in the atmosphere and then replayed it on our station; sometimes we did it live. I also did local play-by-play for softball and basketball and was the program director, too."

Tait was honing his skills, like many others stationed in Sinop. "A number of guys were in broadcasting before they went into the Army," he said, "so we all pitched in. We had two or three guys who were engineers at broadcast stations before they went into the service."

Tait returned to the United States, then was stationed in West Germany for awhile before coming home for good in early 1963. After leaving the Army that August, he got a job at WDZ in Decatur, Illinois, where he was the morning announcer and did the local sports, including play-by-play. In 1966 he began teaching sportscasting at Ohio University. Two years later he joined WBOW in Terre Haute, Indiana, where he was the morning announcer, the program director, and eventually the station manager. At the same time, Tait was the voice of Indiana University football. He was also the studio host for Indiana Pacers basketball, a job that included pregame, halftime, and postgame duties. "I was the Mike Snyder of Indiana Pacers broadcasts," he laughed.

Asked what his career goal was at the time, Tait was blunt. "To stay employed," he said. When Tait read in the newspaper that Bill Fitch was named the head coach of the Cavaliers, he sent him a congratulatory letter. "I'd known Bill on and off for years," he said. "When I was at Monmouth the football team was horrible, and Bill scouted football before he started coaching basketball at Coe College. So he used to kid me about making a 66–0 blowout sound like a 6–6 tie. When I finished my letter of congratulations to him, I wrote at the bottom, 'P.S.—If you ever need anybody to do for the Cavaliers what I used to do for Monmouth College, why, let me know. Ha, ha.' I wrote it, sent it, forgot about it. Fitch called me soon after and said, 'Are you interested in the job?' I said, 'Absolutely.'"

While Cavs public relations director Bob Brown broadcast the team's first eight games of the 1970–71 season, Tait came to Cleveland to do a "test" game. Nick Mileti liked what he heard. The job was his. Asked if he thought he'd be sticking around awhile, Tait was honest if nothing else.

"Well, I couldn't go back to Terre Haute because they sold the station and wiped out the staff, so there was nothing to go back to," he said. "So I hoped that I could stick in Cleveland regardless of what happened. I never thought too much about a future. You just hoped that things would stay alive. The team was not good, the fans were non-existent, and the Cleveland Arena was referred to around the league as 'the Black Hole of Calcutta.'"

Maybe so, but Joe Tait had a job in the NBA. He'd paid his dues and earned it.

5 | The Master Plan

The bubblegum cards were laid out on the family room floor. Bill and Jim hovered over them like a mother bird hovers over her babies. Bill Fitch and Jim Lessig, however, were not collectors of basketball trading cards. Instead, they were ready to pull up their sleeves and go to work. Although Nick Mileti doubled as the Cavaliers' general manager, Fitch and Lessig, believe it or not, were about to do their homework for the upcoming NBA Expansion Draft that would be held on May 11, 1970, and also included both the first-year Buffalo Braves and Portland Trail Blazers.

"Bill brought me with him to Cleveland to be his assistant coach and only scout," Lessig said. "We were in pretty good shape with the college draft because we'd been coaching college basketball and knew the college players. But we just didn't feel comfortable about the Expansion Draft. For some reason, we couldn't get any information on the available players from the NBA. We wanted career statistics and those types of things, but we just couldn't get that kind of information."

Personal computers were not around yet, nor cell phones, not to mention the Internet. "One night in Minnesota," Lessig continued, "my son Tom and I went down to buy some milk or something and he said, 'Dad, can I have a quarter?' And I gave him one. When we got back in the car I looked in the back seat and said, 'Tom, what are you doing?' And he said, 'I'm looking at these basketball cards I bought.' I said, 'Basketball cards? Let me see one of those.' I looked at them, and they were like the baseball cards with pictures of the players on the front and their lifetime statistics—exactly what Bill and I were looking for—on the back. So when I got home, I called Bill and told him about the cards. He said, 'Go back to the store and buy every package of basketball cards they have.' So I went back and spent about $10."

And in 1970 10 bucks bought a *lot* of basketball cards.

"So the next day Bill and I had all these cards spread out on his family room floor," Lessig said. "This was a time when there weren't nearly as many teams, or players, in the NBA, so I think we had about 80 percent of the players on those bubblegum cards."

Fitch and Lessig studied the cards intently during the next two months leading up to the Expansion Draft. Yes, this is how the Cleveland Cavaliers' coaches "scouted" the players who were available—castoffs from other teams—for this dispersal draft. From trading cards!

"We boxed 'em up," Lessig said, "and took them to the Draft in New York City. They put the representatives for Cleveland, for Buffalo, and for Portland in three separate rooms."

In the Cavaliers' room were Fitch, Lessig, Mileti . . . and those bubblegum cards. Each of the 14 existing teams had protected seven players on its roster. After each round, when the expansion clubs selected one player each, the existing teams added another player to their protected lists. The Draft continued until the expansion teams had selected 11 players each, while the existing teams had lost two or three players each. The following are notable players the Cavaliers selected and what they had accomplished in their pro careers:

- Butch Beard, a 6-foot-3, 185-pound point guard who averaged seven points per game in his rookie season the year before with the Atlanta Hawks but, due to military obligations, would not join the Cavs until 14 games into the 1971–72 season
- Johnny Egan, a 5-foot-11, 180-pound point guard from the Lakers who was a serviceable player for four teams in all during nine seasons and who would be traded before the season 1970–71 was done
- Bobby Lewis, a 6-foot-3, 175-pound shooting guard who spent three seasons with San Francisco and who never averaged more than 7.2 points per game
- McCoy McLemore, a 6-foot-7, 230-pound small forward from the Detroit Pistons who played well for a total of four teams during six seasons and who would be traded before the season 1970–71 was through
- Luther Rackley, a 6-foot-10, 220-pound center who averaged 7.6 points and 5.7 rebounds per game in his rookie year with the Royals the previous season
- Bingo Smith, a 6-foot-5, 195-pound small forward who averaged 7.3 points per game in his rookie season the year before with the San Diego Rockets

- John Warren, a 6-foot-3, 180-pound guard who was a rookie reserve on the Knicks the year before
- Walt Wesley, a 6-foot-11, 220-pound center from the Bulls who never averaged more than 9.5 points per game in a four-year career that began with Cincinnati

"John Warren was a hell of a player, a smart player," said Fitch. "He wasn't a power scorer or anything, but he didn't have any real weaknesses either. He was well-grounded in how to play defense. Johnny Egan was a good playmaker. Walt Wesley could put the ball in the basket. He was all 'bring it on!' People talk about 'you throw it in, you'll never get it back' . . . that was Walt. He was a scorer. Luther Rackley was a defender. Bingo Smith was a good pickup for us because he gave us another shooter. If you're going to lose, it's better to lose 100–90 than it is to lose 60–0. The first night of training camp I knocked on Bingo's door to see how things were going. He had a big sandwich and a bottle of red pop in his hands, and he was about 20 pounds overweight. But we got him thinned down and he became famous throughout the league for his ability to shoot what is now a three-pointer. I got McCoy McLemore because we needed a veteran off the bench who could give us some leadership and experience. He was a steady player and was good for what we needed at the time."

Recalled a chuckling Lessig, "We said afterwards, 'We'll never tell anybody that we drafted players by way of what we read on these bubblegum cards.' And we *didn't* tell anybody, at least for awhile. We kept it quiet for a long time."

Some six weeks prior to the Expansion Draft, on March 23, also in New York, the regular NBA Draft had taken place. The first player the Cavaliers ever drafted was John Johnson, a 6-foot-7, 200-pound small forward out of the University of Iowa whom they chose with the seventh overall pick. With their second-round selection the Cavs chose Dave Sorenson, a 6-foot-8, 225-pound power forward from Ohio State University.

"John was certainly an NBA talent," Fitch said. "He had good credentials coming out of college. He played well on both ends of the court. Dave was All-Big Ten, a good talent. We also played him at center."

Two other notable Cavaliers that first season were Bobby Washington and Gary Suiter. Washington, a 5-foot-11, 175-pound point guard whose only professional experience was as a backup for the American Basketball Association's Kentucky Colonels the season before, was claimed off waivers almost two months into the season. Suiter, a 6-foot-9, 225-pound forward, soon to be 26 years old with *zero* pro experience, signed as a free agent 15 days before the season began.

Left to right: **Jim Lessig, Bill Fitch, and Nick Mileti at the Cavaliers' first NBA Draft, March 23, 1970. (Courtesy of AndersonsClevelandDesign.com)**

Needless to say, the 1970–71 Cavs' talent level was about as thin as any expansion team's in NBA history. To the press, Mileti talked about a "five-year plan."

"The reason I said five years," he explained, "was because if you end up last, you get the first or second draft choice once, twice, three, four times, and you're going to start to get some serious talent on that team, and it's that talent that wins and loses games. So that was the principal of the five years. In basketball, with a 12-man squad, playing five at a time, you can do it in five years."

"A big part of Nick's plan was the business side of things," said Fitch, "like how long we were going to be in that old, little building, how long it would take for him to build a new one that he envisioned, and keeping us afloat while we were drawing 3,000 people at the Cleveland Arena. And there was nobody who could make more out of a George Washington than

Nick. Nick and I would put our heads together in terms of if he had the new arena built in five years, where would the team be in competition in five years? The big success wasn't going to come in downtown Cleveland because people just weren't going to come to that building . . . no matter how good we got."

The NBA, back up to 17 teams after a drop-off, was realigned from Eastern and Western Divisions of seven teams each to four divisions within two conferences—the Atlantic and Central Divisions in the Eastern Conference and the Midwest and Pacific Divisions in the Western Conference. The Cavs were placed in the Central Division along with the Royals, Hawks, and Baltimore Bullets.

When he was hired as Cleveland's head coach, the quick-witted Fitch, known for his one-liners, had declared to the press that his name was "Fitch, not Houdini!" The new coach's remark may have merited some laughs, but he was being serious, too, and the team backed him up. With a starting lineup of Egan, Warren, Rackley, McLemore, and Smith, in their first game ever on Wednesday night, October 14, 1970, in front of 7,129 fans in the Buffalo Memorial Auditorium, the Cavaliers were hammered by the Braves 107–92. Smith led the way for the visitors with 21 points. Warren scored 14 and Egan had 12. Two nights later, the Cavs improved and were up by five points entering the fourth quarter but fell 115–112 to the Trail Blazers in Portland, making them zip for two against their expansion brethren.

By the time they returned to Cleveland for their home opener against San Diego, the Cavaliers were 0–7. They fell behind the Rockets 38–17 after one quarter and lost 110–99 in front of 6,144 fans. They went on to lose their first 15 games, including a 141–87 beat-down at Philadelphia on November 2, and had many observers across the country wondering if they would ever win a game. In fact, Lessig recalled one of the New York City newspapers running a contest early in the season regarding the Cavaliers' ineptitude in which readers could win free tickets to a Knicks game.

"Readers," he said, "had to pick the first game in the Cavs' schedule they thought they'd win. So the paper listed the schedule and at the bottom it read, 'Next year's schedule not available.'"

Fitch recalled an amusing story that occurred a couple of hours before loss number 15 to the Warriors at the Cow Palace in San Francisco.

"Normally on the road," he said, "we'd have a bus at our hotel that would drive us to the arena, but our hotel in San Francisco was right across the street from the arena. So I just told the guys, 'Everybody be in the locker room at 5:30, and we'll get dressed just as if we got off the bus and do our normal pregame routine. Get your rest.'"

"So Bill, Joe Tait, and I walked to the arena," Lessig said. "We got to the players' entrance and the security guard said, 'Can I help you?' Well, Joe and I had our identification passes with us, but Bill left his back in the hotel room. So Bill said, 'I'm the coach of the Cleveland Cavaliers.' And the guard said, 'How do I *know* you're the coach of the Cavaliers?' And Bill said, 'You know what the Cavaliers' record is?' The guard said, 'Yes, they're 0–14.' And Fitch said, 'Let me ask you something else. Do you think I'd tell you I'm the coach of the Cleveland Cavaliers if I really wasn't?' The guard smiled and said, 'Go right on in.'"

Perhaps Fitch made the wrong decision by talking himself into the arena that night as his team was pummeled 109–74. Two nights later the Cavs were in Portland for the third time already, believe it or not. Fitch and Lessig went for a walk the day of the game.

"We went by an antique store," Lessig said, "and we saw through the store window a human skull. It wasn't a real human skull, but it was a good replica of one. So Bill said, 'I'm gonna go in and buy that!' And he did. That night, he put the skull on the bench right next to him for good luck."

And the Cavaliers finally broke into the win column by recovering from a six-point deficit after three quarters to beat the Blazers 105–103. Six Cavs scored in double figures, led by Wesley's 21.

"There were pictures all over the country of Bill sitting next to that skull," Lessig laughed.

"The skull stayed with Fitch for awhile but not too much longer," Bill Nichols said.

The losing continued, however. The Cavaliers dropped their next 12 games to fall to an appalling 1–27.

"When it was announced Thanksgiving weekend," Fitch said, "that we'd traded Johnny Egan to San Diego—he'd be returning to California—Johnny's wife ran up to me and gave me a big hug and kiss on the cheek and said, 'Thank you, Coach, thank you.'"

Although the Cavs won their first home game 108–106 over Buffalo on Sunday, December 6, in front of little more than 2,000 fans, things got so bad that three nights later during a home loss to Portland, Warren actually scored a basket for the Trail Blazers! Yes, John Warren scored a basket for the opposition. It happened at the beginning of the fourth quarter off the jump ball at center floor that was customary at the start of each quarter back then.

"We got possession and the ball went to Bobby Lewis," said Fitch. "Lewis fired a beautiful pass to Warren, who went in for a layup . . . but in our basket! And Portland center Leroy Ellis tried to block the shot! And he damn near did!"

Ellis got credit for the points.

"Afterwards," Fitch laughed, "everyone was really riding John and giving him a hard time. The next day I showed film of the play, and the reason I did was because when Warren was going in for the layup, Bingo Smith, who never passed up a shot, was standing over in the corner begging for the ball! All four of them—Warren, Lewis, Ellis, and Bingo—were going the wrong way!"

The Cavaliers fell to 3–37 before winning two straight games for the first time, 120–107 over the Braves at home the day after Christmas and 114–101 over Philadelphia, also at home, the very next day. The win over the 76ers was Cleveland's first victory over a team not from Buffalo or Portland. The Cavs wound up a league-worst 15–67 and in the far reaches of the Central Division basement. They were so futile that their final record was seven games worse than Buffalo's and 14 games worse than Portland's! Even more remarkable was the fact that Baltimore won the Central Division title with just 42 wins but still finished 27 games ahead of the Cavaliers!

"That was one of the worst teams I ever played on," said Smith.

The Cavs certainly had many games in which they were blown out of the gym, but they also had a number of games in which they were more than competitive but folded down the stretch.

"We just didn't have the depth and manpower to finish off," Fitch explained. "Those guys played their butts off, they played hard."

Just how did Fitch keep his players thinking positive through all of that losing?

"The same old way that I'm often thought of," he said. "You work your ass off and never let 'em think they're gonna lose the next game. You play the next one 'cause you're gonna win it. My job was to keep them all thinking and keep them out of the unemployment line. We were all just trying to survive."

Leading the way for Cleveland was Wesley, who was tops on the team with both 17.7 points and 8.7 rebounds per game. The big guy hung up 50 points in a win over Cincinnati on Friday night, February 19. He hit 20 field goals and was 10-of-14 from the free throw line. Wesley's point total was a team record that stood until LeBron James broke it more than 44 years later on March 20, 2005, when he tallied 56 against the Toronto Raptors. Two days after his 50-spot Wesley notched the Cavs' first 20–20 performance with 30 points and 21 rebounds in a loss at Portland.

Johnson, the team's lone All-Star, averaged 16.6 points and a team-leading 4.8 assists per game. He also hauled down 6.8 boards per contest. Others who averaged double figures in scoring were Smith (15.2), McLemore (11.7), Warren (11.5), and Sorenson (11.3).

Steve Patterson reaches for the ball as Walt Wesley looks on in the Cavaliers' 148–119 loss to Philadelphia, January 2, 1972. (The Cleveland Press Collection, Michael Schwartz Library, Cleveland State University)

"That season was just an unbelievable experience," Lessig said. "Being the Cavs' only scout for pros and colleges, I got on a flight about five or six times a week from September through March. I'd go to Seattle, then I'd fly down to San Francisco, then I'd fly down to L.A. to watch UCLA's practice. Because of all the scouting, I wasn't on the bench for too many games, especially road games. We only had six people in the front office—Mileti, Fitch, myself, Bob Brown, salesman Tom Embrescia and Steve Zayac, who was on the financial end."

Not only were the Cavaliers a lousy team, their home, the Cleveland Arena, was perhaps the worst venue in the entire NBA. While it was a showpiece when it opened in 1937, by the time the Cavs came along it had become decrepit and lacked adequate parking.

"When I first got to Cleveland," Smith said, "Bill Fitch picked me up at the airport. He told me, 'I'll take you by where you'll be playing, where your home games will be played.' So he's driving down Euclid Avenue and he stops the car in front of the Cleveland Arena. We get out of the car and I go, 'What's this?' Coming from San Diego and that beautiful arena there to this? I was like, 'Oh-h-h-h ma-a-a-an!' That place was terrible!"

"You had the lights hanging down. It was archaic," remembered Mike Snyder, just a fan at the time but now sports director of WTAM-AM 1100, the Cavaliers Radio Network pregame, halftime, and postgame host, and co-host of WTAM's *Wills & Snyder in the Morning.* "It was a good place for hockey but for basketball it was pretty dark."

"The Arena also had a weird floor, similar to the Boston Garden's with the dead spots and all of that," recalled in 2014 Nate Thurmond, who would join the Cavs later in the decade but who experienced the old, dingy Arena many times as a visiting player for the San Francisco/Golden State Warriors.

"The fans were right on top of you," said Beard. "It was just an old building that was outdated."

"Everybody hated going in there," Thurmond said, "because it was the dirtiest arena in the league as far as the showers and all of that stuff. Everybody used to talk about that mess down there. I used to wear my socks in the shower and then cut them off and leave them there! That's how dirty it was. The hotel we stayed at was right across the street, and we used to dress in our rooms and walk to the Arena in our uniforms because we didn't want to change in the locker room!"

"I used to drive past the Arena and take a left into the parking lot," said Sheldon Ocker. "One time I had to stop because Wilt Chamberlain was crossing the street in his uniform, in his warmups! The home locker room was bad enough, but the visitors locker room was kind of like you would imagine maybe a prison . . . a prison shower room. John Havlicek was the Celtics' player rep I think. One time I was just kidding around when I said something to him about catching diseases in there. He got real upset. He was very upset that you couldn't use the place anymore and you had to register a complaint with the league and those kinds of things. It was bad."

Dave Cowens, Havlicek's Celtics' teammate for many years, believed that the building needed to be condemned. "Oh my god," he said, "that old arena was the worst one ever. It had the worst locker room ever. You had a black mat because the hockey teams played there, so the hockey players came in with their skates on and that mat was just filthy. They had one shower that worked, one toilet and a sink, and if you flushed the toilet while somebody was taking a shower the water would turn scalding hot. The place was terrible. It was cold, too, and I mean out in the playing area. I sat and shivered during a game one time. You'd come out of the game and sit for awhile, and there was no way you'd go back in the game and play full blast because you had to warm up again. They talk about the Boston Garden . . . but that place in Cleveland was the worst."

"You were happy to get in and get out," said Dick Snyder, who would join the Cavs later in the decade but played at the Arena as a visitor many times.

On top of everything else, the Arena was not exactly in the best area of town.

"It seemed like there'd be a car stolen out of the parking lot about once every two games," Ocker said.

"You'd walk out after a game," laughed Beard, "and pray your car was still there."

Not only was the Cleveland Arena tough on visiting teams and the Cavs themselves, Bill Fitch was tough on his players, at least according to Nichols.

"Fitch was a hard coach to play for," he said. "During practices, he'd always get on Sorenson because he never looked like he was motivated and he'd always complain about being hurt. So Fitch would tell Dave, 'You've got to play hurt in this league.' He just ground that into him."

Nichols will never forget an amusing exchange between Fitch and Sorenson during the Cavaliers' first training camp.

"The Cavs," he said, "were playing a rookie game against Buffalo up at Fredonia State College and there was, in Fitch's mind, a bad call. Fitch slams his hand on the table and breaks his little finger. So on the bus ride back to Cleveland Fitch has his hand in a bucket of ice. Sorenson looks at him and says, 'Hey coach.' Fitch says, 'What do you want, Dave?' And Dave says, 'You've got to coach hurt in this league.'"

Lessig recalled Fitch's sense of humor and wittiness saving the season.

"We got national publicity because Bill was so great with the one-liners," he said. "He was such a great quote after the games. He was just unbelievable. I remember the guy who was the promotions director for the Cincinnati Royals at the time calling and saying, 'You guys get more headlines than we do, and we're close to a .500 team!' It was because of Bill. He just carried us through that year. His sense of humor kept that season alive."

"Fitch kept us entertained by telling jokes," Bob Dolgan said.

"He suffered a lot privately from all the losing, though. I could tell," said Nichols. "Defeats hurt him a lot. But he hid it well and would play with the media. He always had a funny line to kind of masquerade all the losing, kind of like [Lee] Trevino did in golf. And everybody loved it."

"Because of that the team became likeable despite its record," said Les Levine, who these days hosts the television talk show *More Sports & Les Levine* but who was just a fan at the time and on through the Miracle of Richfield. "Fitch was the perfect guy to coach the early Cavs teams because he had that sense of humor and he had the ability to learn as the seasons went on."

"Bill Fitch was a wonderful guy to work with," Hal Lebovitz said. "I loved the guy."

"Fitch was also clever, very clever but he was also very calculated and very careful with what he said to us," Nichols said. "He didn't put his foot in his mouth very often. Mileti also handled the losing very well. He was very professional and very positive all the time."

Nichols recalled a humorous story that had to do with Fitch not changing his sports jacket very often.

"When the team came home from a road trip one time," he said, "the team doctor, Nick Sekerak, made up a big can that stood about three to four feet in the air and put a *Right Guard* label on it. He put it directly behind Fitch's chair. They used to have some fun like that."

"One time at the Arena," Dolgan recalled, "Fitch threw a chair because of a referee's call long before Bobby Knight did the same thing when he was at Indiana. Years later Fitch told me, 'My throw was a lot better than Knight's. He slid his chair along the floor. I threw mine on the fly a lot further than he did.'"

"There was a game late in the season we were playing at home," Lessig remembered. "We were down by about 22 points with maybe two minutes left and Bill called a timeout. The players all came over and gathered around him and he was talking and talking . . . and John Johnson said, 'Guys, don't worry, we'll get 'em in overtime.' Bill just looked at me and I looked at him and we thought, 'That's typical of the season.' We kind of became the '62 New York Mets. People around the country followed us because they were interested in the story about this team that couldn't win. It became almost like a cult thing."

Then there was Gary Suiter.

"I don't even know where to start with that guy," Lessig laughed. "Suiter was such a character but he had some ability."

"Gary was quick, strong," said Fitch.

"He had broad shoulders. He was a big dude," Nichols said. "He blocked a couple of Connie Hawkins shots and played pretty well in a preseason game against Phoenix."

"Then he had like 22 rebounds in the second half of an exhibition game against Seattle," Lessig said. "He was phenomenal."

Unfortunately, Suiter's wacky ways trumped whatever abilities he had on the basketball court.

"Oh god, Suiter's a legend," laughed Fitch. "It'd take me too long to tell all the Suiter stories. Scouts looked at him and said, 'Well, he's going to Cleveland to get a look.' I've always told everybody that's how hard up we were."

"Gary Suiter is a book unto himself," laughed Nichols. "When he flew into Cleveland, Ron Culp, the trainer, went out to meet him at the airport. The plane emptied and he was nowhere to be found. Ron said, 'He *has* to be on the plane.' So Ron asked if he could go onto the plane and look for him. So he walked onto the plane and went to the very back and there was Suiter, fast asleep.

"Gary would come upstairs to the press box at the Arena after games all the time and hound me. He'd say, 'You know, if Fitch would play me I could take the team to the NBA title.' Then he'd call both Fitch and Lessig, fake his voice and say, 'You should put Suiter in the game because he could take you to the title. He's a talented player.' This went on and on."

"In the middle of a game at the Arena," laughed Levine, "they found Suiter at a concession stand in uniform and warmups!"

The Cavs finally released Suiter some two months into the season, the story goes, because he was caught rummaging through his roommate's luggage.

"I got a call," Lessig said, "from a funeral director in the Cleveland area the day after we cut Gary and he said, 'Do you know a Gary Suiter?' I said, 'Yeah, what's he done now?' He said, 'Well, he came to our funeral home and told us that his father passed away, and he wanted to make arrangements and asked if we'd let him use our telephone. So we did. We put him in a room and he called every general manager in the NBA to see if he could get a job.' Then Gary would call me constantly and beg me to talk to Bill about bringing him back."

"Then," Nichols said, "Suiter went to the Houston Rockets and got cut three straight days. He just kept showing up. Then the Rockets sent him a registered letter that said, 'Don't ever come back.' Then he was playing in the Eastern Basketball Association—the forerunner to the Continental Basketball Association—and got cut at halftime of a game! Then he was playing in Mexico."

Suiter was murdered on October 23, 1982, near Rio Rancho, New Mexico, following an argument over a gambling debt.

"The guy was just a screwball," Nichols said. "He was different."

With or without Suiter, the Cavaliers were struggling at the gate.

"They were only drawing 3,000–4,000 people most nights at the Arena," Nichols said, "but they just hung in there."

"We gave it a big play, but the city didn't respond too well because the team was losing," said Lebovitz, who was the color commentator on Cavs local television broadcasts that first season and into the middle of the decade. "The fans would turn out when they played the Lakers or the Knicks or the Bucks, but that was about it."

"When I first started covering the Cavs, I didn't go on the road with them," Ocker said. "That's how little they meant then. They weren't important enough. I don't think I began traveling with the team until 1975–76."

"There weren't a lot of fans, but the ones who were there loved the team," said Levine.

"I don't think we ever had a feeling that the Cavaliers were in any danger of folding," said Dolgan. "By then the NBA was a little more established. It wasn't as fly-by-night as it'd been in the late '40s when towns like Syracuse and Sheboygan had teams. Don't forget, Bill Russell and the Celtics had been very popular and the Knicks had those big seasons in the late '60s and early '70s. Everybody felt it was just a matter of time until the Cavs could get the players they needed. We all had a feeling that the NBA was here to stay."

There was one thing the Cavaliers accomplished in 1970–71 that no other team did—they garnered the number one pick in the 1971 NBA Draft. They used it on scoring machine Austin Carr, or "A.C.," as he was known, a 6-foot-4, 200-pound shooting guard from the University of Notre Dame.

"Austin Carr was considered the best college player in the country," Dolgan said. "He was about the most publicized college player at the time. That was really a big plus for the Cavaliers when they got him."

"Obviously Austin was quite an offensive threat," said Fitch.

The Cavs then chose 6-foot-9, 225-pound center Steve Patterson from UCLA in the second round and 6-foot-2, 160-pound shooting guard Charlie Davis from Wake Forest University in the eighth round.

"Steve was a typical John Wooden player," said Fitch. "He knew the fundamentals of the game from A to Z, he practiced hard, he got the most out of the abilities and talent that he had because of hard work. The only thing going against him, besides knee issues, was that he was playing center with a body that wasn't as big as the guys he was playing against night in and night out.

"On our first trip to New York that second season I told the guys, 'I'm gonna make a bed check. You better have your asses in bed. I don't want us runnin' around New York.' So I knocked on every door and the guys were all there except Charlie. I slipped a note under his door that read, 'Charlie, I was here.' And I never said a word to him after that. I didn't punish him. I found out where he was and he was alright."

In the 1972 Draft the Cavs chose 6-foot-8, 220-pound power forward Dwight Davis, or "Double D," as he was known, from the University of Houston in the first round, the third overall pick.

"Dwight had talent, he was a good prospect," said Fitch. "He was a tough guy, too. One time a few years into his career during a home game I turned and said, 'Okay, Dwight, get in there,' and the guys all looked at me and started shaking their heads. They all turned around and pointed up to the stands. Dwight was seven rows up pounding on a guy who'd been heckling him."

Two trades that off-season also helped. One sent Beard to Seattle in exchange for a pair of veterans, 6-foot-1, 180-pound point guard Lenny Wilkens and 6-foot-6, 210-pound small forward Barry Clemens. The other brought 6-foot-3, 185-pound second-year point guard Jim Cleamons from Los Angeles.

"Lenny and Austin made a pretty good backcourt," Fitch said. "Opposing coaches would tell their guards, 'Play to Lenny's left hand, he can't go to his right.' So guys would defend him that way and he'd still go around them. Nobody practiced longer and harder and by themselves as much as Barry did. He and Lenny were inseparable on road trips. They were very close. Barry carried a bag, just an older bag like you carry a sack over your shoulder, whenever he went on a trip. And if you asked him for a doughnut he'd reach into that bag and give you one. If you asked him, 'You got any dice? You got any cards with you?' he'd reach into that bag and give them to you.

"I had some great left-handers and Jim was one of them. He could run a ball club, he knew how to be a leader—in the locker room, on the floor,

With Walt Frazier in the background, Butch Beard pleads for a technical foul call as Dave DeBusschere argues with referee Darell Garretson during the Cavs' 111–109 upset of the Knicks, February 20, 1972. (The Cleveland Press Collection, Michael Schwartz Library, Cleveland State University)

Lenny Wilkens dribbles past the Kings' Nate "Tiny" Archibald, 1973. (Courtesy of AndersonsClevelandDesign.com)

at practices. He was Mr. Smart. If something happened to me and you had questions about the game plan or the scouting report, Jim could answer them probably as well as me."

"Jimmy was definitely a student of the game," said Ocker. "He was also very intense."

The 1973 Draft brought 6-foot-9, 210-pound power forward Jim Brewer in the first round—the second overall pick—from the University of Minnesota and 7-foot, 235-pound center Luke Witte in the fourth round out of Ohio State University. Ironically, and unfortunately, both Brewer and Witte had played pivotal roles in the infamous basket-"brawl" between Ohio State and Minnesota less than 15 months earlier on January 25, 1972, that resulted in a Buckeyes victory by forfeit and hospital stays for Witte and two of his teammates. The two Cavs rookies made peace, however, before the start of the 1973–74 season.

"Jim was the first of the real power forwards for us," said Fitch. "He'd always get the toughest defensive assignment. A lot of nights we'd put him on the opposing center because he was that good at denial. If the center got a shot, he didn't get a second one because 'Brew' had the fundamentals of boxing out and he was second to none when it came to hitting the boards. Jim was also a better offensive player than people give him credit for."

Other notable signings during those early years included Rick Roberson, Cornell Warner, Bob Rule, and Fred Foster. A 6-foot-9, 231-pound power forward and center, Roberson was traded from the Lakers on October 13, 1971. Warner, a 6-foot-9, 220-pound power forward, signed as a free agent on November 4, 1972. Six days later Rule, a 6-foot-9, 220-pound center, was traded from Philadelphia. Foster, a 6-foot-5, 210-pound small forward, signed as a free agent on October 29, 1973.

"Rick had some talent," said Fitch. "He was probably as good a player we had when it came to being hard-nosed, battling, and rebounding. Rick did some good stuff for us. Cornell had some talent, too. We got Bob right at the twilight of his career. He was good to have around, letting the younger guys see what an old-timer could do. Fred was a good player who did well on both sides of the floor."

The Cavaliers slowly and steadily progressed, for the most part, during those early years. They improved to 23–59 in 1971–72 and 32–50 in '72–73 but dropped to 29–53 in '73–74; the latter was Fitch's first season taking over for Mileti as the general manager. Johnson and Beard were All-Stars in 1971–72, Wilkens was an All-Star in '72–73, and Carr was an All-Star in '73–74. Attendance at the Arena rose to 5,222 per game in 1971–72 but dipped a little the next two seasons to 4,548 and 4,013, respectively. Those first four seasons were a learning process not only for the players but also the coach.

"Bill learned as we learned," said Smith. "He learned a lot from Lenny [who had been Seattle's player-coach for three seasons before joining the Cavs] in terms of how to coach in the NBA. To Bill, if you were told to do something you did it. If not, you sat down. But Lenny told him that wasn't the way to coach. He told him to coach more by instinct. And Fitch listened to his advice, at least somewhat."

Rowland Garrett, who would not join the team until early in the 1975–76 season, said that Fitch still had his own way of doing things.

"It was going to be his way or no way, so you had to understand that," he said. "But as long as you played hard and did what you were supposed to do, he didn't have a problem with you. He was fair."

"We didn't have a great season my rookie year," said Witte, "but I just loved Lenny's presence. I can remember him telling me during a timeout, 'He's gonna cock his shoulder when he's ready to shoot. Just watch his shoulder.' And I'm goin', 'I *never* watch the shoulder, I watch the belt,' that kind of thing. And, sure enough, Lenny was right. Just little things like that."

"And," added Smith, "as we kept getting more and more good players we were improving."

6 | Taste of Success

The Cavaliers really acquired some serious talent in 1974. Perhaps it wasn't on the same level as the Pittsburgh Steelers' NFL Draft that same year in which the eventual four-time Super Bowl Champions obtained Lynn Swann, Jack Lambert, John Stallworth, and Mike Webster, all future Hall of Famers, but it wasn't chopped liver either.

Two crucial trades brought 6-foot-11, 220-pound center Jim Chones from the Lakers and 6-foot-5, 207-pound veteran shooting guard Dick Snyder from the SuperSonics, the latter which also gave the Cavs the number eight pick in the NBA Draft, which they used on Campy Russell, a 6-foot-8, 215-pound small forward from the University of Michigan. In the third round of the Draft, the team chose 6-foot, 172-pound point guard Foots Walker from the State University of West Georgia (now the University of West Georgia).

"Chones was at least good in every aspect of the game. He was a tough matchup for teams because he could score in more ways than a typical center back then," said Mike Peticca, just a fan at the time who became a Cleveland Associated Press sportswriter during the Miracle of Richfield season, later wrote sports for the *Plain Dealer* for many years, and now is a freelancer.

"Dick was a guy who'd been around and had a taste of winning more than any of the other guys," said Bill Fitch. "He became kind of a silent leader from the standpoint of being a very intelligent player and an excellent shooter. I always said he had the first quality of an excellent shooter, and that's knowing when to take the right shot. Dick very seldom took a bad shot. He was kind of a Mr. Steady. When we added him, we added stability.

"As for Campy, you'd have to put him on the same level of college notoriety that Austin got when he was drafted. Campy was known for his offense because that's more or less what he did in college. The reason they talked about his offense was because he was so good at it. But if you gave him somebody and said, 'Hey, if you wanna play tonight you guard that son of a bitch, and if he even *looks* like he's getting a free lunch you're gonna be sitting next to me for 48 minutes,' he'd play his butt off.

"Footsy could dribble the ball, he could beat a press, he was a very good assist man, and he could get out and guard people, a lot like [Nate] Archibald. I think he copied a little of how 'Tiny' did things. Footsy was a great practice player, too. He got better every day. He was one of those guys who was loved by his teammates. He was a little guy but a hell of a player."

While Fitch was busy strengthening his roster, Nick Mileti, with partners Howard Metzenbaum and Ted Bonda, purchased the Cleveland Indians from Vernon Stouffer in 1972. Also in '72, Mileti founded the World Hockey Association's Cleveland Crusaders. Later that year he, along with Tom Embrescia and Embrescia's brother Jim, both veteran radio executives, formed Ohio Communications, which purchased both WKYC-AM 1100 and WKYC-FM 105.7 from NBC. Mileti changed the call letters of 1100 to WWWE, or 3WE as the station quickly became known; changed the format from country music to news, talk, and sports; and in 1973 made it the home of the Cavaliers and Indians after both teams' games had been aired on WERE-AM 1300. Mileti also brought pioneering sports talk show host Pete Franklin's *Sportsline* from WERE to 3WE, as 1100, a 50,000-watt clear-channel signal, soon became a sports radio powerhouse.

Two years later, in early 1974, Mitch Gray was 16 years old and living in a small town in Georgia called Tallapoosa, not far from the Alabama border. "There was a daytime-only radio station in nearby Carrollton, Georgia, WLBB on 1100 AM, that was news and sports and maybe some country music in the late afternoon," said Gray, who is employed in Carrollton these days as the sports information director at the University of West Georgia. "I was listening to the station one day and its signoff time was at exactly 7 o'clock, right as *Sportsline* came on WWWE-AM 1100. I became a Pete Franklin fan, I'd listen to Joe Tait call the Cavs games, and I became a fan of the team and a regular listener of the station for years. That's how I found 3WE."

Mileti had his basketball team, his baseball team, his hockey team, his radio stations . . . now he wanted a fight song for the Cavaliers that would be played over the 3WE's airwaves. This is where a gentleman by the name of Larry Morrow entered the picture. A few months after he bought 3WE,

Mileti hired Morrow away from WIXY-AM 1260, or WIXY 1260 as it was known, to be 3WE's morning drive man. "I was absolutely thrilled to death to be working with Nick," Morrow said. "He depended on me. He said, 'Look, Larry, you've come off a big six-year run with WIXY 1260, you're the most popular guy in town, and I want you to take my radio station to the top, which we did. I was thrilled that Nick had that kind of faith in me."

After just 18 months on the job, Morrow had the number-one rated show in Cleveland in his time slot. Things could not have been better for the Detroit native. But they *did* get better.

"Nick was aware that I also wrote jingles," he said. "I'll never forget the day he came to me and said, 'Larry, I want you to write a jingle for the Cavaliers. I want it to be just as good as 'Sweet Georgia Brown' is for the Globetrotters.' I said, 'Oh, no pressure there, Nick!' So I wrote the song. It was called 'Come On Cavs—Got to Make It Happen.' I told Nick, 'It's so good I'd like to record it in New York, but it's gonna cost probably $10,000 to do it.' He said, 'I want you to do it.' So I went to New York and recorded the song with some of the best singers and musicians there. I brought it back and Nick loved it. He said, 'I'm gonna take it into the meeting and play it for the [Cavs'] board [of directors].' He called me after the meeting and said, 'I played it for the board.' I said, 'Well, what was it like?' He said, 'You could hear a pin drop. Nobody said anything.'"

The board members thought the song was too soulful for that time, but in the end it turned out to be a smash hit. Some 10,000 copies of the record album were sold.

Everything seemed to be coming together . . . like a perfect storm. The Cavs were thought to be ready to contend for a playoff berth. Their games would now be broadcast on a radio station that reached, as 3WE itself proclaimed, "38 states and half of Canada." There was now a "groovy" team fight song that was upbeat and catchy. The team even had new uniforms, with the classic block lettering and checkerboard pattern on the sides of both the jersey and shorts. What else was left? How about a new arena?

From day one when he purchased the Cavaliers, Mileti knew the team would not survive in the Arena, that dingy disaster of a building on Euclid Avenue. He had a vision from the very beginning of building a state-of-the-art arena for his team and for the fans. "Nick had a great allegiance to the local people," said retired *Akron Beacon Journal* sportswriter Tom Melody.

Mileti was eying little Richfield Township in Summit County for the structure that he would call The Coliseum. "I remember going to cover the Richfield council meeting and meeting Nick Mileti the night he presented his proposal to build The Coliseum in Richfield," recalled Melody. "He had

Larry Morrow with the record album "Come On Cavs—Got to Make It Happen," 2010. (Courtesy of AndersonsClevelandDesign.com)

his plans and told the council members, 'This is what I want to do but I'm not forcing myself on Richfield.' He told them, 'Here are the tax benefits' and so on and so forth. Nick was a showman, there isn't any question about that, and I say that in the very purest sense. I think this was one of the ways into the spotlight, and he obviously did the Akron area an incredible favor by feeling that way."

Once the Richfield council voted to allow The Coliseum to be built and all the i's were dotted and t's were crossed, it was time for the builders to get to work—right on State Route 303, just to the northwest of Interstate 271, almost exactly halfway between Cleveland and Akron, some 21 miles from each city. "I think when Nick did his study of where to put The Coliseum," Melody continued, "one of the things he looked at was where the people were and how long it would take them to get there. I also remember he had some other reporters and myself to the site while The Coliseum was being built. We put on the hard hats and went through and saw what they were doing."

What they were doing was constructing what turned out to be a palatial edifice, with all the amenities—the main arena, two full-sized practice courts, a weight room, loges, suites, office space, and more. The late Jim Swingos, owner of the famed Swingos Hotel in downtown Cleveland, which had a classy restaurant, even opened a second restaurant in The Coliseum! The Coliseum was quite simply a spectacular venue. Some four years after it opened, in 1979, a *Sports Illustrated* article proclaimed, "No arena was more beautiful than The Coliseum, a magnificent structure in Richfield, Ohio."

"That building," said Fitch, "was light years ahead of all the buildings that had then been built. You couldn't ask for a better building. There are a lot of arenas that have been built since then, including the one the Cavs are in now, that aren't as good as that one."

"It was like a dream come true!" Bingo Smith declared. "It was the best arena in the whole NBA."

"I begged Mileti not to build it out in Richfield," Hal Lebovitz admitted. "I wanted it downtown and I fought it, but when I went out to see it when it was built I thought it was a beautiful thing."

"It was a heck of a novelty," said Melody. "I mean, suddenly, Akron is almost looking at itself as being a pro basketball town. And some of the players even lived down that way."

The huge, white building did have its detractors. Visiting players and writers, broadcasters, fans, and even some of the Cavs players were not too keen on its location. "It was a wonderful building," said Jim Cleamons, "but we all thought it was too far away."

"It was out in the middle of nowhere," Les Levine said. "While it was a gem of an arena, it wasn't accessible. There was no good way to get there from the airport, from downtown Cleveland, from the suburbs."

"They promised there'd be public transportation—buses—to The Coliseum from both Cleveland and Akron, but there never was," said Fitch.

"That made it extremely difficult," Bob Dolgan said, "to get out of The Coliseum parking lot after games with big crowds."

"And certainly the nightlife wasn't what everyone would've liked it to be," said Levine.

"The area around The Coliseum never really grew," Melody said. "Other than a Holiday Inn that was already there, there were no new motels. There were no shopping opportunities. There were a couple of restaurants that

The Coliseum, spring 1975. (Courtesy of AndersonsClevelandDesign.com)

were already there but no new ones. Granted, this wasn't conveyed the night of that council meeting, but it's possible that there was no growth around The Coliseum because the people of Richfield just wanted to be left alone, didn't want any industry out there."

According to Dolgan, there was no doubt that Melody's hunch rung true. "The people in Richfield did everything they could to prevent The Coliseum from being built," he said. "They wanted to maintain that country atmosphere. The funny thing is, 25 years later when The Coliseum was being torn down, those same people were trying to *prevent* it from being torn down. And five years before that, they did their best to keep the Cavaliers from moving back to Cleveland."

Nonetheless, with the Cleveland Arena closed down, to be demolished three years later, when The Coliseum opened with a sold-out Frank Sinatra concert on Saturday night, October 26, 1974, it was a big deal, a very big deal. "It was a pretty neat thing," Melody said. "It was just a hell of a thing is what it was."

Two nights later Stevie Wonder sold out the joint. Muhammad Ali fought Chuck Wepner there in March of the next year in Cleveland's first major boxing match in 44 years, a bout that inspired the movie *Rocky*. At a time when the rest of the United States laughed at Cleveland, Mileti had come to the rescue and put the city on the sports and entertainment map. Thousands of events would be held at The Coliseum.

When it opened, The Coliseum's seating capacity for basketball was 20,273, the largest of any NBA arena at the time. "They were all pretty good seats, though," said Mike Snyder, "even the ones that were real high up."

When the Cavaliers christened their sparkling, new arena with their first home game on Tuesday night, October 29, they had by far the most talent of any Cavs team in the franchise's brief history. More than 13,000 fans showed up to watch their new and improved basketball team take on the defending NBA Champion Boston Celtics, whom the Cavs had beaten by one point in "Beantown" just six nights before as part of their 3–3 start to the season. Despite 20 points from Smith and 19 from Austin Carr, an awful third quarter was the difference as Boston won 107–92.

The Cavs won three straight games to improve to 6–4 and less than a month later they were 13–8. They were 22–18 after beating the Sixers 108–106 in the Spectrum on January 18. They seemed to be Team Streak as an eight-game losing skein ensued, but then they won 10 of 13 to improve to 32–29 as postseason dreams danced in their heads. Then they lost seven straight, and the playoffs seemed to be slipping away. But then they won seven of

In a crucial contest for both teams, the largest crowd ever to watch an NBA game to date—20,239—cheers the Cavs to a 100–95 victory over New York, April 3, 1975. (The Cleveland Press Collection, Michael Schwartz Library, Cleveland State University)

10 to get to 39–39 with four games left. They lost at Houston and Atlanta but returned home for their Coliseum finale, an April 3 meeting with the New York Knicks, who were battling for an Eastern Conference playoff spot themselves. A then-NBA record crowd of 20,239 showed up and cheered the Cavaliers to a 100–95 victory. Snyder scored 16 of his 22 points, and Cleamons tallied 17 of his 19, in the second half to bolster the Cavs.

The Cavaliers needed to win their finale against the Kings three days later on a Sunday afternoon in Omaha, Nebraska, to qualify for the playoffs and end the regular season with a 41–41 record. They were down 29–27 after one quarter, 51–45 at halftime, and 78–75 after three quarters. They fought to within a point at 95–94 with three seconds to go. The season came to a heartbreaking conclusion when Fred Foster's shot from the top of the key was blocked as time expired. "Fred should've passed the ball to me," said Smith. "I was supposed to have taken that shot."

It was a disappointing end to a season filled with hope. The fans seemed to be buying into the team's improvement as average home attendance jumped to 8,161. "We really seemed to be meshing," Cleamons said.

"Austin Carr had averaged more than 21 points per game in his first three seasons combined," said Peticca. "During the first half of the '74–75 season he was scoring at right around the same rate and I'm thinking, 'This guy right now is one of the top two or three shooting guards in the NBA.' Then he hurt his right knee badly and missed about half the season. Then, later in the year, guys like Cleamons and Chones had injuries, not as serious as Carr's, but they still missed eight or 10 games. There were a couple other injuries, too. And the team finished just a game out of the last playoff spot. I think the last couple weeks of the season, when every game was critical to making the playoffs, was an experience that helped the Cavs get used to the big-game atmosphere."

An atmosphere that would truly arrive the following season.

THE
SEASON

7 | Nate Comes Home

By the time the 1975–76 season arrived, the Cavaliers' starting lineup looked like this:

- Jim Cleamons, point guard
- Dick Snyder, shooting guard
- Jim Chones, center
- Bingo Smith, small forward
- Jim Brewer, power forward

"Austin Carr was now coming of the bench backing up Snyder, and Footsy Walker backed me up," Cleamons said. "The beautiful thing behind this—and I give A.C. all the credit in the world—was that Austin saw what was happening and he didn't fight it. He saw his value, and his ability to score, as our sixth man. He didn't complain, he accepted it. He didn't fight the chemistry and that really helped our basketball team. And he was also still getting his numbers. We now had offense in Dick as the starter and we had offense in Austin coming off the bench. And Campy Russell, a great scorer, backed up Bingo.

"The best thing the Cavaliers did was that they put people together who had one thing in mind, and that was trying to win games. And it was my job to see that that got taken care of. I was the groove that kept everything going because I was unselfish with my distribution of the ball."

The Cavs got off to a rough start in '75–76 by losing four of their first five games, three by nine points or more. Road wins over the Atlanta Hawks and New Orleans Jazz were followed by close defeats to Houston, defending NBA Champion Golden State, and Seattle to drop the team's record to 3–7. When the Cavs fell 98–94 to the Chicago Bulls on November 25, their record was 6–10.

Foots Walker goes for a layup as Campy Russell and Luke Witte wait their turns during a practice session at The Coliseum, fall 1975. (The Cleveland Press Collection, Michael Schwartz Library, Cleveland State University)

"I thought the '74–75 Cavs were a nice team, better than their record," said Mike Peticca, "so I was disappointed when the team started the '75–76 season the way it did. The roster was basically the same. I think a lot of times things don't really pan out as to how a season is going to go until you're a couple of months into it. I think also maybe roles were changing a little. Footsy, Chones, and Campy were rookies the year before, so when they came back for '75–76 maybe early in the season Bill Fitch was still trying to figure out the exact roles . . . guys were adapting."

"That happens sometimes," Chones said. "We were still very young so we had some growing to do."

Smith believed the unusually long exhibition schedule played a major role in the Cavs' rough early going. "I think some of the players, even myself, were kind of worn out," he said. "We played exhibition games all the way up until the day before the start of the regular season."

Fitch, along with assistant coach Jimmy Rodgers, knew that something had to be done, that a change was needed, that his team needed a spark. Come Thanksgiving Day, Cavaliers fans not only had family, food, and football to be thankful for, they were also grateful for the addition of a future Hall of Famer to their favorite team's roster. Nate Thurmond was his name, reviving the Cavs his game. A living legend and a veteran of 12-plus seasons in the NBA, including two Finals appearances, not to mention a native of Akron, Thurmond, along with backup forward Rowland Garrett, arrived in town by way of a trade with the same Bulls team that had beaten the Cavs two nights earlier in which Chicago received backup big men Steve Patterson and Eric Fernsten. The 6-foot-11, 230-pound Thurmond was brought in to serve as a much-needed backup to Chones.

"At the time we picked Nate up," said Nick Mileti, "I felt that our basketball team was playing better basketball than what we'd been playing the year before when we actually finished the season strong and missed the playoffs by just one game. And there wasn't really anything we could do to get better other than pick up somebody to replace the one weakness I thought we had, and that was when we took Jim Chones off the floor we became an inferior basketball team for six or seven or 18 minutes, depending on how long we kept Jim off. And if we continued to play Jim 40 minutes we still weren't going to make it up. We were eight minutes short at the center position, and we were going to have a tired Chones. So what Nate gave us was a full 48 minutes of top center play."

"If we could get 30–31 minutes a night out of Chones, nobody was any better than him for that period of time," Fitch said. "And then Nate cleaned up. That's the way we did it. I think Chicago thought Nate was probably done. He was playing the same amount of minutes with the Bulls as he wound up playing with us, but they didn't win games because they had him. They won games because of who they had playing ahead of him. They used him a lot different than we wound up using him. On top of that, Nate was coming home! I thought that was the whole key. If you bring a guy home and he gets a chance to play in front of the home people, you don't have to give him a pep talk every night."

"It wasn't like a great drop-off in talent when Thurmond went in the game," Tom Melody recalled. "Plus, he was a very inspirational type of person, and I think sometimes we tend to work harder when we're around somebody of his stature who's just a very good person with a towering reputation for basketball. I think that probably helped. I think just having him there . . . I mean, how are you gonna dog it when you've got a guy like Nate Thurmond out there killing himself? You can't do it."

"I think seeing somebody of Nate's stature come to a team like the Cavaliers that hadn't been that successful helped and motivated a lot of guys on the team, especially Chones," Snyder said. "They saw a guy his age who was limited physically by a long, hard career and what it'd done to his body play all out, play team ball every time he went on the floor rather than go through the motions."

"Jim finally had a teammate who he could relate to as a big man," Cleamons said. "Nate offered advice to him on how to become a better player, defensive positioning, and how to play certain people. And Jim took that mentorship to heart. It just worked out well. It was also a good combination because Jim was offensive-minded and Nate gave us a wonderful defensive presence."

"There's no question Nate's presence helped," said Les Levine. "The Cavs had practically nobody who had any playoff experience. For the most part, they were young guys. It was only the sixth year of the team. It was new to everybody. It was new to the front office, it was new to the coach. Thurmond was arguably the biggest name that the franchise had had at that point from a success standpoint. He was somebody the players all looked up to."

"Nate had experience, he'd been through the wars," Chones said, "but he also had some game left in him and he proved that with us."

Thurmond was also a very humble person. "Despite all that he'd accomplished in his career Nate felt he had to earn everyone's respect," Snyder said. "That's just how he looked at it: 'Hey, this is a new situation. I don't care what I've done in the past, I want to go out there and show these guys I can play.' I think that came from inside Nate. He didn't have to earn my respect, he'd already done that. That's just how he approached the game. If he had a new situation, he wasn't going to embarrass himself. He was going to go out there and prove he could still play."

"I think the players had a lot of respect for me for what I'd done in my career and they listened to me," Thurmond said. "I didn't try to take over in any way as far as talking or playing, but I certainly tried to do a little bit of both. That second unit that I was on, we kept the lead going and sometimes would expand it. And then at the end of the game, usually with about seven or eight minutes to go, I'd always come in and we were able to keep maintaining the lead. I was able to solidify the defense on the second unit, and that was what we needed."

"I was in awe of Nate when I first saw him try to pick up a guard off a pick and go out there and try to block the guy's shot . . . 22, 23 feet from the basket!" proclaimed Snyder. "Not many centers would do that. But he'd pick up that guard and he'd play him defensively like he was a guard! He wasn't going to back off and say, 'Hey, go ahead, I'm gonna give you this shot.'"

"Just by watching Nate I was able to pick up how to guard certain players, guys who used to kick my butt," Chones said. "Now, they were afraid of me. I'd watch what Nate would do—his demeanor, how he passed the ball, how he stretched out his game. He didn't try to do everything in the first few minutes. He just knew how to play. He was an old-school center who had a lot of pride, who believed in rebounding and blocking shots. He ran the floor, he set picks, he just had experience, experience I didn't have, so he was perfect for me because I could measure myself by him. I had a chance to practice with him every day, and I watched him and learned a lot from him."

Backup center Luke Witte had opposed Thurmond several times before and said he was no doubt one of the toughest players he ever faced. "Nate," he said, "had those long arms and didn't let you go very many places."

"Cleveland was still a young NBA city," said Peticca, "and Thurmond was the first guy who made the ordinary fan appreciate what defense meant at that level."

Thurmond commanded respect when he walked into a room. He was a huge presence, literally and figuratively. "You figure anybody who's 6-foot-11 or 7-foot has a presence but it was different with Nate," Sheldon Ocker said. "He had a presence of . . . an authority figure . . . how a [military] general was supposed to look and act and give off this kind of aura. There was just something special about Nate when he walked by. Even if he walked by with a whole bunch of tall guys you'd look at him and say, 'That guy is one of the leaders of the team.'"

Thurmond possessed A-plus people skills, too, and proved it when he approached Witte.

"Luke was a big, affable guy," Thurmond said. "I was at the end of my career, and I felt maybe he could learn some things from me because certainly I wasn't going to be with the Cavs very long. And I thought he had the size to be a serviceable player. So I tried to let him know that I probably was going to take some of his time but that he had time to wait, so to speak."

Recalled Bob Dolgan, "Thurmond just wanted to make Witte feel at home, let him know that he wasn't the famous player joining the team who was going to look down on a guy on the bench, not even talk to him or anything. And it not only made Witte feel better, it made everybody feel better. It was just that kind of attitude Thurmond had."

"Nate was such a gracious guy, a great guy, an absolutely great guy," Witte said. "I was hoping for more playing time. Everybody does. But you get a guy like Nate, a signature ballplayer . . . I was excited about that, but I knew what that would mean for me. Just the way he handled himself, though, was really cool."

Thurmond thought his new team was talented but simply did not believe in itself. "The players just didn't have any idea how good they were," he said. "They were relatively young with some veterans splashed in there. They weren't positive-thinking. I'd been on quite a few teams over the years, and I could see a lot of talent as far as at each position, offensively and defensively."

Smith recalled a meeting Thurmond had with his new teammates soon after his arrival.

"Nate said, 'Look, man, you guys don't know what you've got here,'" he said. "'You started off slow, so let's pick it up and win this thing!'"

The Cavaliers lost four of their first six games after the trade. Then they got hot and reeled off seven straight wins—the longest winning streak in team history to that point—to improve to 15–14. The team was really beginning to jell, as evidenced by the fact that the first five wins of the streak were by 14 points or more. The Cavs would never dip below the .500 mark again that season.

"Nate was the catalyst as far as I'm concerned," said Snyder.

"All of a sudden, the team's inside defense got a lot better," Ocker added. "They had a guy who was the last line of defense who they didn't have before. With Nate in the middle, if Snyder or Cleamons or Bingo or whoever was playing tight man-to-man defense and their guy got past them, Nate was now standing there. They didn't have to play like 50 feet from their

The 1975–76 Cavaliers. (Courtesy of AndersonsClevelandDesign.com)

man and worry about the guy getting around them and going to the basket. So that made a huge difference. Also, I think the other players began to understand the concept of working harder on defense better."

"Just the way Nate anticipated things, he helped us learn just by watching him," Witte said. "He wasn't the player he once was, but he was still *really* enthusiastic about the game and enthusiastic about being with us."

"You didn't see Nate that much," Levine said, "but whatever minutes he played he gave everything he had."

Thurmond recalled two turning points for him personally during the '75–76 season. The first one took place at the end of the Cavs' final victory of their aforementioned seven-game winning streak, at home against the Los Angeles Lakers on December 21. "It was nearly a packed house, I'm going against Kareem [Abdul-Jabbar], and we're winning by one point with about 15 seconds to go," Thurmond said. "L.A. called timeout. Everybody in the gym knows the ball's going into Kareem. It did. And, although I didn't block his shot, I was able to defend it well, made him shoot a hook shot that he didn't want to shoot, and it was off. And after the shot, the buzzer went off. People started screaming, 'We beat L.A.!' That gave me some credibility among my new teammates that 'he can play some defense.'

"The other turning point came about two months later up in Buffalo. I got fouled on a layup or something and went to the line with us leading by one point late in the game. I needed to hit two free throws to clinch the win [there was no three-point shot at the time]. Now, I hadn't been in that position too many times. New teammates, I'm concentrating, thinking, 'I gotta get these,' and I made both free throws and we won the game.

"Those two moments, in my mind, helped me be able to talk to my teammates and for them to listen. I felt I needed to prove myself a little bit. Everybody can hear what you did, but they want to see a little bit of what you can do."

The Cavaliers may not have been the best team in the NBA in 1975–76, but they were quite possibly the deepest. "Eventually," explained Peticca, "Fitch got that great nine-player rotation where coming off the bench you had Walker at point guard, Carr at shooting guard, Thurmond at center, and Russell at forward. What was cool for the fans was that after that settled in you could almost know when those guys were going to come in and when the starters were going to come back."

"It was almost set in stone," Thurmond said. "I've got to give credit to Fitch. He knew how to use his players."

"Once they started to jell, all nine guys in that rotation," Peticca said, "as a fan, you knew what that guy was counted on to do, and you also had a lot of confidence that that particular guy would excel in that role."

"We'd grown together as a team," said Cleamons. "We knew each other's tendencies, we accepted each other's roles, strengths, and liabilities. We had great chemistry."

"Fitch told me I'd be playing 20–22 minutes a game at the most," Thurmond said. "He told me that he wanted me to get some rebounds, block some shots, set some screens, and I'd pick up some little garbage rolls into the basket, and that's just what it turned out to be."

"The styles of the first and second units were different," said Peticca. "When you'd bring in Campy, Footsy and A.C., I think they'd look to run more. They were more athletic. Also, any combination of the three big guys—Chones, Brewer, and Thurmond—you had a pretty good defensive rim protection. Chones was a good defensive player, but, boy, when you had Thurmond and Brewer on the court together, wow, that was terrific defense! I thought the way Fitch put together that rotation and stuck with it was great coaching. And, no matter what circumstances, he stuck with it and it sure paid off. I also thought that team—actually all of Fitch's Cavs teams—were very good coming out of timeouts."

"We could take a full timeout and bring in the next wave of players," said Smith, "and we didn't miss a beat."

"Fitch had a great vision for that team," Thurmond said. "He did a great job with that."

"When we substituted I didn't think we fell off," Fitch said. "The thing that made that ball club was the chemistry the players had with one another. I never looked at our second 'wave' of players—Walker, Carr, Thurmond, and Russell—as 'backups.' That team really got by on a lot of nights because of who they were as a group, not who they were as any individual."

"I thought Fitch was an excellent coach," Dolgan said. "There's no doubt his strength was handling people. He always said, 'The secret to being a good coach, a successful coach, is to keep the six guys who hate you apart from the six guys who aren't sure.'"

Thurmond acclimated himself to his new surroundings with ease because everyone got along and there were no egos. "Everybody was scoring the same amount of points," he said. "There weren't a lot of guys on the bench who were mad because most of the guys were playing. And the couple of guys who were not playing didn't seem to mind. They worked hard in practice."

"Fitch," said Melody, "was an extremely intense person on and off the court. He was a bit of a pugnacious person I would say, but the thing I remember most about Bill was looking at his eyes one time toward the end of a season, and they were literally blood red from watching film. He was extremely dedicated to his profession. I remember looking at him and thinking, 'What else is there to see? He's played this team 10 times. How could you still be watching film all night and this and that and the other?' I was just amazed that that late into the season somebody would still be watching film that much. I just kept thinking, 'There are only 10 guys out there, there are only so many ways to play basketball. How could there still be more for him to learn?' He was a good coach. I think he was a good x's and o's coach and a good players' coach. I think he really understood the whole picture. I think he understood that he had to be the boss. I don't think we'd yet reached a place where players started 'coaching.' I think he was still the boss, but I think there was a great deal of respect for him probably because of how hard he worked."

Fitch said continuity was crucial to the Cavs' success. "We could've probably traded for a player," he said, "who was better than any one of our guys, but we kept that group together unlike many teams in this day and age. Our guys were so tight-knit that if I were to have broken that up, it would've cost us because the chemistry factor was that important. And the fans . . . God, I think if I'd traded Austin Carr or Dick Snyder or any of those guys, hell, they'd have probably burned my house down! Those fans were in love with that group, and that's so important."

Levine likened the '75–76 Cavaliers to the early 1970s New York Knicks teams that won NBA titles in 1970 and '73. "At almost every position the Cavs were not quite as good as those Knicks teams," he said, "but it was still a very similar team. The Cavs were deeper than those New York teams, but New York's starters were better. Jimmy Cleamons was not a great player but for that Cavs team he was terrific. All of those guys on that Cavs team were perfect pieces to the puzzle that year."

The '75–76 Cavaliers may have been without a single All-Star, but they had seven players who averaged double figures in points, with Chones leading the way at 15.8. The others were Russell (15), Smith (13.6), Snyder (12.6), Cleamons (12.2), Brewer (11.5), and Carr (10.1). Brewer was the team leader with 10.9 rebounds per game. Chones was next with nine boards per contest. Cleamons led the Cavs with 5.2 assists per game. Defensively, Cleveland yielded just 99.2 points per game, which ranked second in the league.

"It was the ultimate team," Snyder said. "There were some guys on that team like Cleamons, like 'Brew,' of course, Nate when he got there, and to some extent myself who really understood their strengths and weaknesses and, for the most part, tried to play within the framework of those strengths and weaknesses. I think there were a number of guys on that team who realized that that was the only way they could play. For example, for me to get points we'd have to be running where I'd be on the break and hitting

Bingo Smith prepares to shoot against the Bucks, February 13, 1976. (Courtesy of AndersonsClevelandDesign.com)

layups or transition jump shots, or there'd be set plays that would call for me to come off a pick. I wasn't good enough with the ball to make my own points. We had a very structured offense. I could score when we ran if we had someone out there like Foots Walker who was going to distribute the ball on either the break or the secondary break.

"Campy and Bingo were sort of the wild cards. You pretty much knew what everybody else out there was going to do when they got the ball in certain situations. But Bingo and Campy were the guys on the floor who you weren't quite sure whether they were going to break the play one-on-one or

Nate Thurmond defends Kareem Abdul-Jabbar, March 16, 1976. (The Cleveland Press Collection, Michael Schwartz Library, Cleveland State University)

. . . both of those guys felt like they had the ability to get the shot off. It wasn't a selfish thing or anything. In other words, they'd get the ball, they'd see an opportunity and they'd take it, even if it was a situation where maybe they were supposed to catch the ball and then make the pass back to the point and make a cut. You can liken it to an audible by a quarterback in football."

That seven-game winning streak the Cavaliers put together was halted the day after Christmas in a 98–97 loss to the visiting Hawks. They rebounded to win three straight games over defending Eastern Conference Champion Washington, Buffalo, and Kansas City before losing three straight to Philadelphia and Detroit twice that dropped their record to 18–18 on January 7. It would be the Cavs' last three-game losing streak of the season. It would also be the last time they stood at the .500 mark. The team won three of its next five games before really turning it on and reeling off five straight wins and six of seven. Then on February 1, heading into the All-Star break, they blew a seven-point halftime lead in losing a heartbreaker at New Orleans 96–95, a game in which "Pistol" Pete Maravich of the Jazz scored 36 points. The Cavaliers stood at 27–22, one game behind 28–21 Washington.

"Coming out of the All-Star break I didn't know if we could win the Central Division," Thurmond admitted, "but I thought we were pretty good."

The Cavs changed Thurmond's mind when they reeled off eight straight wins, raising their record to 35–22 and inching into first place in the Central Division with the Bullets hot on their trail. Thurmond remembered Cavs fans, who showed up that season to the tune of 12,659 per game, coming to the realization that their pro basketball team was no longer an also-ran but a serious contender to not only qualify for the playoffs but perhaps cause some damage once it got there.

"The fans were going wild," he said. "We were rolling, we were taking all comers. Cleveland hadn't experienced this type of situation and most of the players themselves hadn't experienced it, so everybody was giddy but everybody was professional about it."

"They were football fans," Chones said. "Basketball was not as publicized in Cleveland. People were not as familiar with it, and that includes the writers, so we didn't get that much publicity. The Cavs had been losing ever since their first season. They'd been a joke for the most part. So when we started winning people said, 'Hey, look, there's a story here!' The writers started doing interviews and doing stories on the players and the coach and Nick and . . . after a while it caught on and there was a lot of curiosity and there was some interest, and people started coming to the games. And the games were cheap—for five and seven bucks you got a darned good seat. This was all new for Cleveland. It'd always been football, but now they had some reason to cheer for basketball."

It was nip and tuck between the Cavaliers and Bullets the rest of the way. The Cavs lost four of their next six games to fall out of first place. They got back on track, though, with a 110–99 victory over the Warriors on March 11 before nearly 20,000 fans at The Coliseum. That pushed them to 38–26 and pulled them within a game-and-a-half of 41–26 Washington. Ten days later, led by Smith's 27 points, the Cavaliers won their 42nd game of the season—clinching their first-ever winning record—with a 95–92 triumph over the visiting Bullets before 20,784 screaming fans. That improved their record to 42–28, but they still stood a game-and-a-half behind the boys from D.C.

It may have taken a year longer than Mileti had planned, but on March 31 the Cavaliers clinched their first-ever playoff berth with a 110–101 victory over the Jazz in the Superdome. Four wins in their last five games, including a 101–92 triumph over the Celtics in Hartford, Connecticut, on April 6, gave the Cavs the division title by a single game over the Bullets, 49–33 to 48–34. Cleveland's record was the third best in the NBA and second best in the Eastern Conference, the latter which made them the second seed in the five-team conference playoffs. While fourth-seeded Philadelphia battled fifth-seeded Buffalo in a first-round, best-of-three series, with the winner to face top-seeded Boston, the Atlantic Division champ, the Cavs' opponent in the second round would be none other than third-seeded Washington, a team they defeated four out of six times during the regular season but also a team loaded with postseason experience.

"We knew that to win in the playoffs it was a whole different ballgame," said Smith. "We had to learn how to win in the postseason. It was win or go home."

8 | Bedlam and the Bullets

The uneasy Cavs hosted Washington in Game 1 of the Eastern Conference Semifinals on April 13 before 19,974 fans. The Bullets scored the first eight points and raced to a 20-point lead while hitting 12 of their first 14 shots. The Cavaliers came back but, with Elvin Hayes tallying a game-high 28 points for the visitors, fell short 100–95. Jim Chones led Cleveland with 23 points.

"I've got to believe the Cavs were prepared for the intensity of the game because they had a lot of big games down the stretch," said Mike Peticca, who was in attendance. "But I also have to believe that they very well might've had some jitters. Thurmond was the only team member with any valuable NBA postseason experience. I think the jitters might've affected the shooting as much as anything because the Cavs couldn't hit anything. You could sense a little disappointment from the crowd. The final score is really deceiving. It was never that close."

"If you're going to bet on a Game 1 forget about where it's being played," said Bill Fitch. "Usually the first game of a series is almost like it's being played at a neutral site because nothing's happened yet to make the crowd go one way or the other. And experience usually wins that ball game, and Washington was a much more experienced basketball team than we were. And I'm talking about the experience of playing that game number one.

"The thing that we did, though, was that we learned by coming back. When you come back like that, it gives you confidence. We knew what we had to do. We looked at the films and so forth and we just figured, 'If we do this and everybody is on the same page we're gonna win Game 2.' The one thing that we sold to our players was, 'Every game against these guys could go either way because that's how evenly matched we are. If we're not the best team in the league at this point of the season, they are. Forget about the Bostons, forget about the Golden States. If we're healthy and they're healthy, Washington or Cleveland is the best team in basketball at this stage of the season.' And we were."

Although the 2-2-1-1-1 venue format was popular back then, two others used in those days were odd—1-2-2-1-1 and, believe it or not, 1-1-1-1-1-1-1. The latter was used for the Cavs-Bullets series. Thus, Game 2 two nights later would be played in the Capital Centre in Landover, Maryland. Because of that, Peticca believed it was a must-win for Cleveland.

"Washington was such a good team," he said. "They'd been swept by Golden State in the Finals the year before so their motivation had to have been sky high, while the Cavs were still trying to get their feet wet as a playoff team."

Miracle Number One . . .

The score was tied at 24 after one quarter. The Cavaliers trailed 46–36 at halftime before bouncing back to tie the game at 63 after three periods. They were down 79–74 late in the game when Chones hit a turnaround 10-footer to pull them within three with 1:21 remaining. After Washington's Dave Bing misfired on a 15-foot jumper, Jim Cleamons connected on a 20-footer with 1:02 left to make it 79–78. The Bullets brought the ball up the court then called timeout with 51 seconds to go. A three-second call on the home team with 41 seconds left gave the ball back to the Cavaliers. A walking call on the visitors, however, gave it back to Washington. Bing palmed the ball, giving the Cavs possession again with only six seconds left. Fitch called timeout.

"Coach told me to take a shot anywhere I could get it," Bingo Smith said.

From mid court Cleamons inbounded the ball to Smith, who launched a 25-footer . . . Bingo! The Cavs were up 80–79 with two ticks left on the clock. Smith was reasonably confident the shot was good when he let it go.

"That was my range!" he said.

The Bullets, who were led by Phil Chenier's game-high 19 points, called timeout. Then from mid court Wes Unseld inbounded the ball to Hayes, who spun, shot it, and missed. The Cavs had evened the series at one.

"Bingo's shot just changed the whole atmosphere of the series," said Peticca, who watched the game on television with friends.

"That win really gave us some confidence," said Smith, who led the Cavaliers with 17 points.

"That shot is why Bingo's in the lore," said Mike Snyder, who was just out of college and working as a disc jockey at a radio station in Oberlin at the time. "It was all part of that building up to . . . even though it happened on the road, that's what really turned The Coliseum upside down, when they came back in that game. That's when it really started to take hold."

Game 3 would be back in the cozy confines of The Coliseum on April 17. A then-NBA record—and raucous—playoff crowd of 21,061 was on hand.

"The fans were so pumped up with that first playoff win under their belt," recalled Peticca, who attended that game, too. "I just think the Cavs' defense, especially, really fed off that. Their defense was just *crazy* good in that game. You look at that Bullets roster . . . Elvin Hayes could do so much down on the block, he had a bit of a face-up game . . . he and Wes Unseld were on the boards . . . you had Phil Chenier and Dave Bing with all they could do offensively. I mean, they brought guys off the bench like Nick Weatherspoon and Clem Haskins. They had a lot of ways they could score. The Cavs' defense in that game—and really throughout the series— was just stifling. Both teams, actually, played great defense the whole series. I think in most playoff series NBA teams play as hard as they can defensively, but that Cavs-Bullets series was so intense as far as defensive efforts, it was tough to score. And that was a defensive era!"

Austin Carr hit four of five shots and seven of eight free throws as the Cavaliers raced to a 45–37 halftime lead. The Bullets kept it close in the third quarter despite eight points from Dick Snyder. The Cavs, though, put it away in the fourth as they were up 73–58 with 8:17 left. After a missed shot by Washington's Truck Robinson, Carr drove to the basket and scored to make it 75–58. Jimmy Jones came back and made a 12-footer, but Chones banked one in to make it 77–60. After Chenier misfired, Smith connected from the corner to increase the home team's lead to a monstrous 19 points at 79–60 with 6:19 to go. The Cavs put it in cruise control the rest of the way, sailing to an 88–76 victory, the second straight game they held the Bullets to less than 80 points. Carr and Smith led the way for Cleveland with 17 points apiece. Hayes led Washington with 17.

Four nights later in Game 4 at Landover, despite 22 points from Campy Russell and 21 from Chones, Haskins, a veteran guard in his final season, came off the bench to score a team-high 22 points in helping the Bullets to a 109–98 triumph after the game was tied 51–51 at the half. The series was knotted at a deuce apiece.

Miracle Number Two . . .

The next evening, on April 22, it was back and forth in front of a boisterous Coliseum crowd of 21,312, another NBA playoff record, breaking the "old" mark set by the Cavs just five days earlier. The game was tied at 23 after one quarter. Washington led 49–48 at halftime. Snyder hit seven of 12 shots and two free throws to keep it that close. The Cavs were up 76–71 after three quarters. Washington tied it at 78. The score was 86-all when Hayes made one of two free throws with 1:48 remaining. A tip-in by Jim Brewer off a Cleamons miss put the Cavaliers up 88–86 with 1:24 to go. Hayes hit from a short distance, was fouled, and completed the three-point play to give the Bullets an 89–88 lead with 1:12 left.

After a Cavs timeout, Snyder connected from the top of the key to put Cleveland up 90–89 with 50 seconds to go. Chenier hit over Snyder from the right side to give the visitors the lead right back at 91–90 with 36 seconds remaining. Soon after, Snyder tried to pass the ball inside, but it was knocked away by Unseld and picked up by Hayes. The Bullets could have killed the clock, but Hayes, who led Washington with 25 points, was fouled by Russell with seven seconds left. With the three-point shot still four years away, the "Big E" had a chance to put the nail in the Cavs' coffin with two free-throw attempts.

"I had a car problem," Peticca remembered, "so I had to listen to that game on the radio. You're thinking, 'Aw man, they're gonna be down 3–2.'"

Hayes, though, missed the first free throw amid a deafening din. He missed the second one, propelling the fans into an even bigger frenzy.

"Elvin Hayes," Mitch Gray said, "was one of the greatest offensive players of all time. He couldn't guard a parked car, but he wasn't out there to guard a parked car. He was un-guardable, and the fact that he missed those two free throws . . . it was like winning the lottery."

Smith's take on Hayes's missed free shots? "He was known to do that from the line anyhow," he laughed.

After Hayes's second miss, Brewer rebounded the ball and the Cavs called time with six seconds remaining. From center court Snyder inbounded the ball to Chones, who was fouled by Unseld as the Bullets had one foul left to give. With five seconds to go, Snyder, who scored a game-high 26 points, inbounded the ball to Smith. Smith dribbled and threw up a running, off-balance jumper that missed by a mile. The ball fell right into the hands, though, of Cleamons, who was running to his left underneath the basket just to the right. Without even taking a step, Cleamons reached to the left and tried a reverse bank shot that sat on the rim—for minutes, it seemed—before falling through the net as the clock hit 0:00. Final: Cavaliers 92, Bullets 91. It was madness as the fans went wild.

"They went crazy!" said Smith.

"Joe Tait's call on that was just spectacular," Peticca said.

"Other than maybe Johnny Most's 'Havlicek stole the ball!' that's my favorite NBA call ever," added Gray.

"I remember I was sitting in the front row behind the basket behind the hockey boards," Les Levine recalled. "You didn't have floor seating in those days like they have now. The first row was actually behind the hockey boards. And at the end of the game I remember just going nuts, and I looked down and there I was standing on the hockey boards, and I have no idea how I got there!"

As for his shot that landed in Cleamons's hands, Smith had a different take than most observers. "Everybody says it was an air ball but it was actually a pass!" he proclaimed. "I mean, how could I make a 25-footer [in Game 2] then on a 15-footer hit nothin'? Come on!"

"I *hope* Bingo said that tongue-in-cheek because that was not a pass," Tait chuckled.

"Bingo's shot a pass?" Cleamons laughed. "He was shootin' that baby."

"We won, so it doesn't matter to me what everybody says!" Smith declared.

"Bingo and I were very close," Cleamons said, "and because of that I knew he was going to shoot that ball. And my instincts told me if he missed it I might have a chance to tip it in. So I followed my instincts.

"We still needed one more win, though, to close it out."

Four nights later in Landover, the Cavaliers fell behind by 17 points in the first half. Carr and Russell, though, got hot as they cut the margin to five at 49–44 at the intermission. The Cavs were down by 10 late in the third quarter, but Chones and Brewer scored to cut the deficit to six points heading into the fourth period. By the time Cleamons nailed a 20-footer with 2:02 to go, the game was tied at 88. Relentless defense on both sides resulted in zero points for the rest of regulation. Overtime followed. Quick baskets by Jones, Chenier, and Unseld rattled the Cavs, who were held scoreless for the first three minutes of the extra period. Speaking of Unseld, Chones said the Bullets' big man was one of the toughest centers he ever played against: "Wes was an undersized center but was very wide."

The visitors refused to quit, cutting the deficit to 96–92 with 1:33 remaining. Then, after an air ball by Jones, Thurmond got the rebound and fired the ball to Russell, who passed to Carr. Carr, who led the Cavs with 27 points, drove to the basket and scored to pull his team within two points at 96–94. But then Hayes, doing his best to atone for his two missed free throws in the late stages of Game 5 by leading all scorers with 28 points, hauling down 13 rebounds, and blocking eight shots, connected from the left of the lane over Thurmond. The Bullets went on to win 102–98, forcing a deciding seventh game.

Miracle Number Three . . .

It was back to The Coliseum on Thursday, April 29—a night that Cavaliers fans will never forget.

"All the stories about the noise are not exaggerated," Peticca said. "I got there really early and I'd say at least an hour before the game it was so loud. And that was without the help of a scoreboard like today prompting the crowd on. I mean, it was real noise, totally fan-generated, nothing to do with any scoreboard or cheerleaders or mascots. Before the Cavs came out to warm up the fans yelled over and over, 'We want the Cavs! We want the Cavs!' And when they *did* come out to warm up, the place just went nuts."

It was a nip and tuck affair the entire way with lead changes galore—16 of them—and neither team able to forge far ahead. Neither club led by more than seven points. The Cavs were up 23–19 after one quarter and 48–47 at the half in front of yet another NBA record playoff crowd—this time 21,564.

"The Cavs were down by four or five points in the mid- to late-third quarter," Peticca recalled, "and I was concerned, thinking, 'Man, the way these teams are playing defense and as intense as this is, even a couple more Washington buckets could expand that lead to eight, nine, 10 points. Then it'd really be tough.'"

It didn't happen. Snyder tied the game at 71 a half-minute into the fourth quarter. Hayes hit a shot from the top of the key, but Thurmond made a two-foot hook shot to tie it again at 73. Bing scored on a driving layup, then Hayes laid one in off a rebound to give the Bullets a 77–73 lead with 8:37 to go. Brewer hit a 20-footer to make it 77–75, but Chenier came right back with a bucket to make it 79–75. The Cavs then reeled off eight straight points, including two great shots by Cleamons, to go up 83–79. Weatherspoon and Jones scored to knot it at 83 with 2:02 left. Snyder then rebounded his own misfire from 12 feet and put it in with 1:38 to go for an 85–83 Cavs lead.

A loose ball foul on Cleamons with 1:31 left put Hayes at the line. With Hayes's two missed free throws late in Game 5 seven nights earlier still fresh in their minds, the fans by now were causing an uproar that nearly blew the roof off of The Coliseum. With nearly 22,000 boo birds sounding more like 22 *million,* Hayes missed the first free throw. The crowd erupted. He missed the second one. The crowd went crazy. Russell, though, turned the ball over, but a three-second call on Washington gave the ball back to the Cavaliers with a minute left. Snyder drove to the hoop, but his shot was blocked. Two tip-ins missed. Jones grabbed the ball, then passed it up court to Weatherspoon, who threw it out to Unseld. The Bullets' big man passed it to Chenier, whose 15-footer from the wing tied the score at 85 with 24 seconds to go and also gave him a game-high 31 points.

Timeout Cavs. Cleamons inbounded the ball to Thurmond from under his own basket. Thurmond passed it back to Cleamons, who brought the ball up the court. He dribbled around until the Cavs called time again with nine seconds remaining. From mid court, Cleamons inbounded the ball to Snyder, who was 20 feet out on the left side.

"I was going to catch the ball and shoot the jump shot," Snyder recalled. "That was the play we set up. But rather than Phil Chenier guarding me they had Wes Unseld come out, so I didn't have the open jumper."

Snyder stayed left, drove past Unseld, and banked in a running, one-handed shot from five feet away with four seconds left. Snyder said the shot was, no doubt, a prayer.

"As I was driving I was too close to the baseline to have any kind of angle to bank it in with my left hand," he said.

So Snyder, the thinking man's player, switched hands and shot the ball with his right one. His basket sent the partisan crowd into mass hysteria.

"It was incredible," said Snyder, who led the Cavs with 23 points. "It was the loudest crowd I'd ever heard."

"The first thing I thought was, 'What's next?'" laughed Peticca, who was as worried as could be when Washington called time. "I was afraid of an inbounds pass down on the block where Hayes would score, get fouled, and make a foul shot to *win* the game, not just tie it."

It was high drama.

From mid court, Unseld lobbed the ball toward Hayes in front of the Cavs' basket, but the Big E tripped and fell. Snyder knocked it free, Chenier chased it down, grabbed it, and hurled up a prayer from the right corner. It missed. Game, set, and match, Cavaliers. Final score: Cavs 87, Bullets 85.

"That last four seconds seemed like the longest four seconds ever! It had to be *eight* seconds," laughed Levine. "What hometown clock person doesn't start the clock early?"

With "Come On Cavs" blaring in the background amid a thunderous roar, hundreds of fans rushed the court. The Cavs' basket stand was torn down.

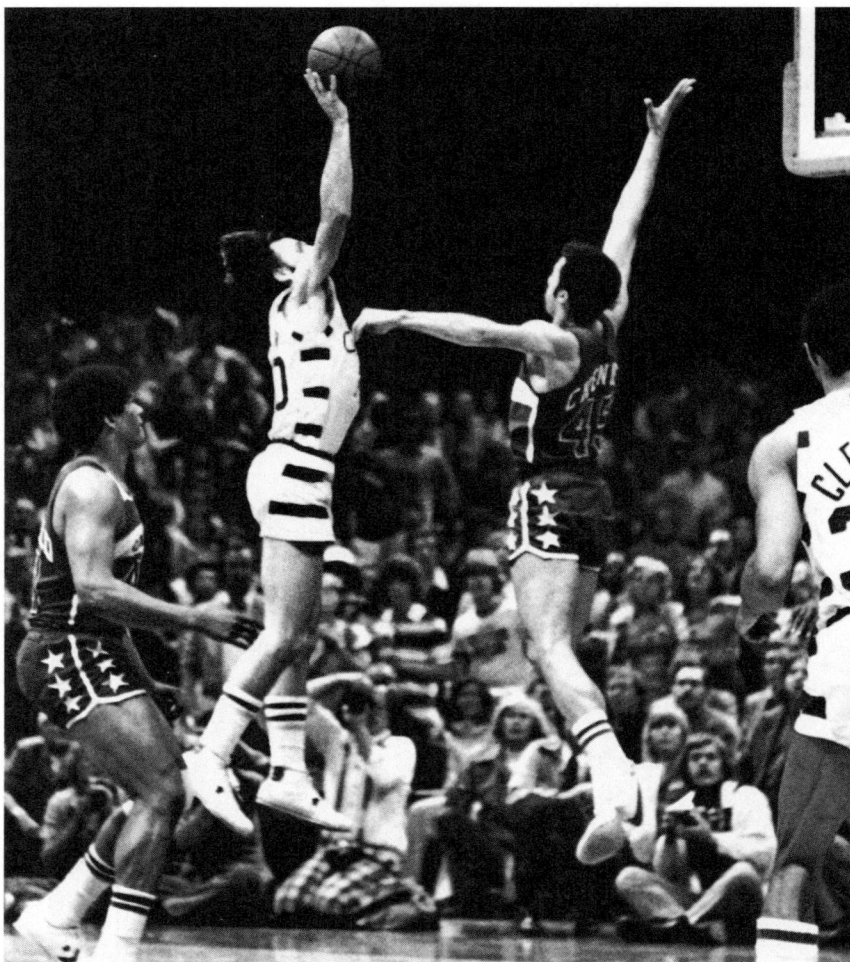

Dick Snyder banks in the winning basket against the Bullets in Game 7 of the Eastern Conference Semifinals, April 29, 1976. (Courtesy of AndersonsClevelandDesign.com)

It was complete euphoria. The Cavaliers were on their way to the Eastern Conference Finals against the winner of the Boston-Buffalo series, which was tied at two games apiece.

"The place just went nuts," Peticca said, adding that he was not one of the fans who celebrated on the court. "It was the cheapest seat, I think five dollars. I was behind the basket on the Cavs' bench end of the court way, way up in the rafters. I just remember I stayed there as long as I could just enjoying it until most of the people were gone. I was just trying to take it in because . . . it was really cool! I was born in 1952 and the Indians had not been in contention since 1959, and the Cavs were still relatively new.

And the atmosphere being inside an arena, it's so intimate compared to, say, a football game. I just remember thinking, 'Man, this is great to be here! I wish every *regular-season* game could be like this.'"

The noise level was so deafening that it actually shook The Coliseum.

"It was pandemonium," Fitch said. "I've never coached in a louder atmosphere than that entire Washington series actually. It was something. But when Game 7 ended, it was just complete joy and happiness. It was a thing of its own. You knew that you were part of something that you were never going to see again. You couldn't duplicate what went on that night. And you couldn't duplicate that noise. Those fans were the same poor bastards who broke their tails getting to that old arena. They were all massed out there at The Coliseum. That was their coming of what they all prayed for and wanted to happen. And they deserved it. No fans ever deserved something like that more."

Although the excitement on the court was, for the most part, just plain jubilation, Tait recalled that the security guard in front of him was in grave danger.

"This poor fellow got knocked down in the stampede," he said, "so my engineer and I both leaned over the table—while I was on the air!—and pulled him back to his feet so he wouldn't be seriously injured . . . or killed!"

"You couldn't hear yourself. It was deafening . . . from the beginning of the game to the end," recalled Charlie Strasser, the Cavs' athletic trainer, equipment manager, and traveling secretary from 1974–80, who is now retired and lives in the Houston area. "I think that's why we won. They talk about the 12th man in football. I don't know what you call it in basketball, but I think the fans really picked the guys up."

Tom Melody remembered it well. "Those fans could shake that building, they really could," he said. "I don't know that I ever heard a noisier place except perhaps when the Minnesota Twins were in the World Series in 1987 and they made so much noise in that dome of theirs that they blew out the computers we were using at press row."

"It was electric. You almost couldn't stand the noise," Hal Lebovitz recalled. "My wife stopped going with me because she couldn't stand it. It was just . . . these days, the fans get to the games at game time or a little later. During those '76 playoffs, they were there long before tipoff and you could just feel the atmosphere was magnetic."

"One time," said Bob Dolgan, "Fitch was giving a talk to the players before a game, and the fans were yelling so loud that his chalkboard supposedly fell down off the stand because it was so noisy!"

Thurmond recalled Fitch having to hold huddles closer to mid-floor because of the noise.

"By the bench where we usually had our huddles you couldn't hear," he said.

Lebovitz brought Buddy Bell and Duane Kuiper as his guests for the deciding game against Washington.

"They both asked, 'Why can't this happen to the Indians?'" he said.

"I play a tape of the crowd noise from the Washington series when I'm feeling down for a morale boost," said Thurmond, whose brother recorded the games.

"It's *still* the loudest I've ever heard," said Smith. "I haven't heard anything even close to that."

"The place just shook. It was ear-shattering," Levine said. "It was the loudest venue that I've ever been in."

"The building was all concrete, so the noise just echoed in there," said Chones. "I remember standing next to Campy Russell talking with him, but we couldn't even hear what the other person was saying. We had to scream at each other."

"I was up in the stands with my friends," Mike Snyder said, "and you just couldn't communicate with one another."

"Almost every game of the series was a surprise. There was tension from the opening whistle until the final whistle," said Levine, who also recalled Tait struggling big-time as the series progressed. "All of his yelling while describing the action gave him a very bad sore throat."

Tait said it was a genuine outpouring from the crowd.

"There was no technical augmentation and things of that nature like there is today," he said. "It was just genuine fan response from 20,000 people."

"It was all very spontaneous," Mike Snyder said. "The crowd was just into every play. The excitement . . . went right through your body. I got chills. Each game was like an event, and it got better each time. As big as that building was, it was so loud that it seemed like you were in a smaller arena."

"After the games," Dolgan said, "it was so tough to get out of the parking lot that a lot of people would just go upstairs into the bar at Swingos and watch replays of the games—the whole game!—and they'd be yelling and screaming all over again."

"The replays would have Tait's calls to go along with them," said Levine. "The fans would stay up at the bar while the parking lot emptied a little bit. I think for the first game we tried to leave right afterwards and got stuck, so for the rest of the games we'd actually make plans to stick around and watch the replays."

"We never wanted to leave the building," Mike Snyder said. "We'd just stay around and have a beer. It was just a big party. Everyone was in a good mood, just loving it, and couldn't wait until the next game."

Levine continued, "I also remember Pete Franklin doing his radio show from a glassed-in booth in the concourse and hundreds and hundreds of fans standing around and listening."

"The Arbitron numbers for Larry Morrow's show on 3WE the morning after games were, I believe, like nothing you'd ever seen before," Mike Snyder said. "Larry would play highlights—Tait's calls—of the games from the night before. People who'd listened to those games would turn off their radios before they went to bed and leave it on 1100 so they'd wake up in the morning to Morrow talking about the game and playing the highlights."

"A nine or 10 share is considered to be a big number," Morrow said. "I was told there was a period during the Miracle of Richfield in which my show registered an 80 share, meaning if two million homes in the Greater Cleveland area had their radios turned on then 1,600,000 of them were tuned in to my show. It's still probably the highest share that's ever been registered in Cleveland radio. It was incredible."

Speaking of Tait, he will go down as one of the finest basketball announcers of all time.

"Joe Tait," Peticca said, "was as good and as exciting a play-by-play guy—and we've had some great ones in Cleveland in all sports—who we've ever had. He might be the standard by whom all the others are measured. I remember even in those early years you didn't miss anything that happened on the court. He'd never say, 'Rebound Cavaliers!' which other announcers occasionally say. He'd say, 'Rebound Brewer!' You knew who made the pass to set up the baskets. He was so precise in his play-by-play. He really understood the tempo, the flow, of the game and what was significant and what was just ordinary as far as how a game developed. He had a great sense of when to let his excitement show through. With Joe, you knew when something mattered most."

"I thought Joe was terrific," said Levine. "Just the longevity tells you how good he was and how the fans loved the guy. Even though the team wasn't very good in the beginning, he was so exciting that people would tune in just to listen to him."

Said Cleamons, "When the games were on television fans would turn the TV down and listen to Joe's play-by-play while they were watching the game. That's how much they thought of him."

The accolades just kept coming.

"Joe's the best ever," Chones said. "There's nobody close."

"I've been associated with two great announcers—Joe Tait and Bill King with the Warriors," Thurmond said. "Those two guys could describe a game and make you feel like you were there. Joe had a great feel for the action. He had a great voice, too. He wasn't a homer but was exuberant about the Cavs."

Joe Tait (*left*) and Pete Franklin circa 1976. (Courtesy of AndersonsClevelandDesign.com)

"Soon after discovering 3WE and Pete Franklin," said Gray, "I discovered Joe Tait. He was the best play-by-play man in the NBA and I became a big Cavaliers fan."

Tait was not without a sense of humor.

"I remember a game we had down in Houston," Luke Witte laughed. "There were like six people there. It was pathetic. And I heard Joe say while on the air, 'I've got Luke Witte standing in front of me. Luke, how many people are here?' He'd do stuff like that all the time. He was just a fun guy to be around."

Tom Hardesty, who was just a young boy but an observant one at the time and is now the assistant sports editor of the *Record-Courier* in Kent, may have said it best: "Joe Tait *was* the Cavs."

Asked if the fact that Cleveland's two other major professional teams, the Browns and the Indians, were not exactly title contenders, to put it mildly, had anything to do with the fans' craziness over the Cavaliers, Thurmond said perhaps a little.

"The Browns' and Indians' problems probably added to the juice," he said, "but when you get 20,000-plus people to an arena and you have a good team and you have some squeaky close games against a great team, that's more than enough."

Witte remembered himself and the rest of the Cavs' players attaining rock-star status.

"You couldn't go anywhere in Cleveland without having people stop you," he said. "I remember one day Dick Snyder and I were driving home from practice—we lived in the same apartment complex—and we stopped at Mc-

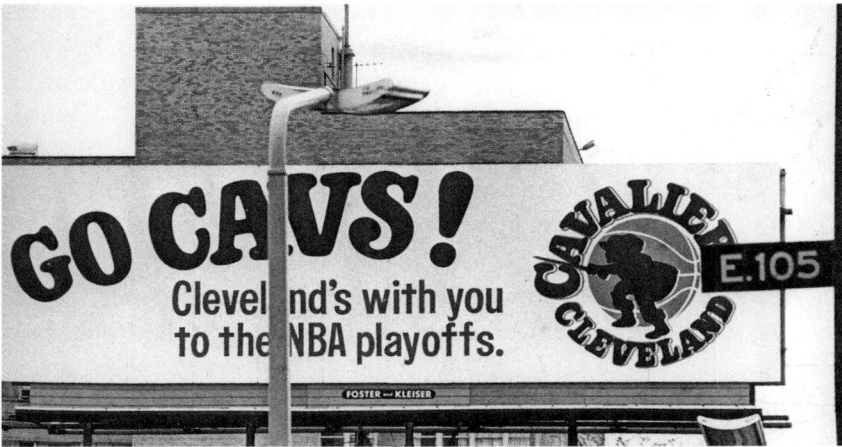

Cavs fever was rampant during the 1976 playoffs as evidenced by this sign at East 105th Street and Chester Avenue. (The Cleveland Press Collection, Michael Schwartz Library, Cleveland State University)

Donald's or Burger King. The workers there said, 'Order whatever you want. Just go ahead and have a seat. We'll bring it to you.' Then one of them took some kind of mega speaker outside and announced, 'We have Dick Snyder and Luke Witte here. Come on in!' It was just a zoo! It was great!"

"It was so much fun," said Peticca. "I've covered Indians home games in two World Series and I've covered Browns playoff wins . . . but that seventh game against the Bullets . . . that was just . . . and I was still just a fan. I'd just begun covering the Indians, but from a fan's standpoint it was about as good as I've ever been a part of."

"I was on the floor at 'The Q,'" Mike Snyder said, "when LeBron hit that shot at the buzzer against Orlando in '09, and I was on the floor when the Cavs beat the Pistons to go to the Finals in '07. There were some thrilling Browns playoff games in the late '80s. And the Indians crowds in the '90s were something to remember for sure. But nothing was quite like the Miracle of Richfield crowds. That was in its own class in terms of that kind of atmosphere. It was . . . it was just . . . you had to be there."

"I'll never forget the Miracle of Richfield," said Cavs fan Mark Jacim, who these days lives in Tampa, Florida. "I was 11 years old at the time, living in Garfield Heights. I listened to every game on the radio. Joe Tait's calls were unforgettable, from Bingo Smith's jumper to Jimmy Cleamons's lay-in to Dick Snyder's shot. It was incredible! I purchased the *Miracle in Richfield* album and must've listened to it 200 times! Listening to Mr. Tait scream to the point of hoarseness after all those last-second wins never failed to give me goose bumps, and still does."

To those who may have felt that the better team didn't win, that the Cavs got lucky against the Bullets, Chones said that is a bunch of bologna.

"The best team wins in a seven-game series," he said. "We were better than them. That's why we beat them. There's no such thing as 'we should've won' or 'they got lucky.' I believe in facts. And the fact is, we beat them so we must've been better than them. To me, it was obvious. They had some guys with big names but we played better. We played better as a team, we made baskets, we stayed aggressive, and we were the better team."

"To win that series . . . the Bullets had Elvin Hayes and Wes Unseld! They were the team! They were a huge favorite in that series," Mike Snyder said.

"They had great guards, too," said Cleamons.

"The Cavs, though, were just so locked in and they fed off the crowds," Mike Snyder continued. "And Washington really didn't have an answer for the kind of bench the Cavs had. You could see that there was something real special with that group."

"In my mind it was validation of how far we'd come as an organization," Cleamons said. "It was, and is, a sense of pride because you go from being the laughingstock of the league playing in that old arena in front of 3,000–5,000 people to playing in The Coliseum in front of more than 20,000 people. The odds are not in your favor at certain times, but you diligently work and are persistent in what you're doing, and now here you are moving on to the conference finals. There's a lot of pride there."

Proclaimed Hardesty, "People started to believe that team could do anything!"

Thurmond agreed. He felt the sky was the limit for that 1975–76 Cavs team. "I thought Washington was the best team left when we beat them," he said. "I felt we had a good shot at going all the way."

Three days after they eliminated the Bullets, the Cavaliers learned who their next opponent would be—Boston. The Celtics beat Buffalo 104–100, winning that series in six games. Even though the Celtics-Braves series was still hot and heavy the night the Cavs had ousted Washington, Fitch had an inkling who would reign supreme.

"As I was running off the court," he said, "I was probably already thinking about Boston."

9 | "Broken" Hearts

The Cavaliers had gone 2–3 against Boston during the regular season, so they knew they could play with the Celtics, and even beat them. This was a very good Boston team, which had finished with a 54–28 record, the second-best mark in the NBA behind Golden State's 59–23 record, but it was not necessarily on the same level as some of the legendary Celtics teams from their storied past.

The Cavs got a big dose of just plain bad luck on Tuesday, May 4—a 6-foot-11 dose of it. In a practice session at The Coliseum two days before the opening game of their best-of-seven Eastern Conference Championship Series against the Celtics in Boston, Jim Chones broke his right foot. The Cavs' starting center was done for the season.

"Jim was running down the court and just came up limping," Charlie Strasser recalled. "He didn't think he broke anything at the time. We thought he might've sprained an arch, something of that nature. We took him for precautionary x-rays to the office of one of the team physicians and he saw a stress fracture. It was a freak injury. Jim had no contact with anyone. A person that tall and that powerful . . . if the right type of torque and pressure is put on something, it can happen. I believe it was his fifth metatarsal, the outside bone."

Chones avoided surgery but did have to undergo rehab to ready himself for the next season.

"It was a shame because Jim was having one hell of a year," Strasser said. "He was at the peak of his career."

Not only had Chones been the Cavaliers' leading scorer during the regular season, he was also their top points producer in the playoff series against Washington at 15 per game. It was a major blow, to say the least, for a team that had come so far. It also meant that 34-year-old Nate Thurmond would have to carry the load at center.

"I knew we were in trouble," said Bill Fitch, who was named the NBA Coach of the Year. "Nate knew he was going against probably the best young center in the league at the time in Dave Cowens. To ask Nate to go 30–31 minutes a game against Cowens was asking a lot. But I felt he'd do well. Nate never disappointed me."

"I remember the disappointment I felt when I heard that 'Chonesy' had broken his foot," Mike Peticca said. "You knew that would put a huge burden on Thurmond."

"It broke my heart because Chones was our main man," Bingo Smith recalled.

"It was definitely a letdown . . . for the entire team," Thurmond admitted. "I knew we were missing a big part, that I couldn't replace Chones offensively. He was such an integral part of what we were doing. During the season he was shake 'n bake and get them tired, and I'd come in there and finish 'em off. So we had to get some more points somewhere. I had to start fresh and step up is what it amounted to. I had to play a lot more minutes, but that didn't bother me. I still felt we had a shot to beat Boston."

"I hate to sound like a typical Cleveland sports fan," Mark Jacim said, "but I am one and we've been through the ringer no doubt. My very first experience with the heartbreak of Cleveland sports was when I heard the news of Chones's injury. As a young boy, I was crushed by how unfair it was that we'd have to play Boston without one of our best players. I still remember how upset I was. This was the start of a long, painful love affair with Cleveland sports for me."

Chones's injury also meant more minutes for Luke Witte, who suddenly was thrust into backup center mode. The tall, blonde-haired former Buckeye was ready.

"I had to be," he said. "Nate needed rest."

"I felt we should still beat them," Chones said.

Despite all the mystique surrounding the hallowed Boston Garden and its unique parquet floor, and with their crutches-laden starting center on the bench, the Cavaliers did not seem fazed in Game 1 on Thursday night, May 6. In Thurmond's first start as a Cav, he and his teammates fought the Celtics tooth and nail to a 77–77 deadlock after three quarters. Thurmond played 39 grueling minutes and finished with nine points and 16 rebounds, but the Cavs lost 111–99. John Havlicek scored a game-high 26 points. Dick Snyder and Campy Russell each scored 21 for the Cavaliers.

In Game 2 three days later Cleveland raced to a pair of nine-point leads and had a 73–70 advantage early in the fourth quarter. But Havlicek, Cowens, and Charlie Scott combined for 11 straight points to put Boston up 81–73. The Cavs cut it to 83–81, but the Celtics stretched their lead to 89–81 on the way to a 94–89 triumph. Smith and Snyder each scored 16 points. Jo Jo White of Boston led all scorers with 24. The Cavs trailed two games to none heading back to The Coliseum.

"I could tell that my team was missing me in its rotation," said Chones.

On Tuesday night, May 11, 21,564 screaming fans showed up for Game 3, which would turn out to be a tremendous defensive struggle. The Cavaliers led 43–38 at halftime, at which point Thurmond had held Cowens to just eight points. The Cavs kept the lead until Paul Silas hit two free throws with 9:56 left in the game to tie the score at 62. Jim Brewer tipped in Smith's missed 18-footer to put the home team up 64–62, and after a missed shot by Scott, Austin Carr, who came off the bench to score 17 points, hit two free shots to make it 66–62. An offensive goaltending call on Cowens off a White hook shot was followed by a 25-footer by Smith to increase Cleveland's lead to 68–62. An 18-footer by Carr with 1:01 to go gave the Cavaliers an 80–72 lead that was too much for the Celtics to overcome. The Cavs, who were led by Jim Cleamons's 18 points, went on to win 83–78. White scored a game-high 22. Cleveland was right back in the series, down two games to one.

In Game 4 on Friday night, May 14, the Cavaliers put on quite a show for another throng of 21,564. They played perhaps their finest game of 1975–76, and quite possibly, in their short history. It was a titanic struggle until the eight-minute mark of the fourth quarter. That was when the Cavs began a stretch in which they turned a 79–77 lead into a 97–83 advantage, finalized on a Russell drive to the basket for two with 2:20 left. Cleveland wound up winning 106–87. Smith led all scorers with 27 points, hitting a sizzling 13 of 17 field goals. Carr and Cleamons chipped in with 16 points apiece while Thurmond added 12 points, eight rebounds, and six awesome blocked shots. White led the Celtics with 23 points. The series was now tied 2–2, but the next game would be back in Boston two days later.

A foot injury he suffered in Cleveland kept Havlicek out of Boston's starting lineup in Game 5. He would see action only if it became critical. And critical it would become for the Celtics. The game was another frantic battle, with the Cavs up 23–22 after one quarter and the score tied at 42 at the half. Thurmond, who was doing a masterful job on Cowens, picked up his fifth foul early in the third quarter. He played with caution until fouling out with 5:03 left in the game. Soon after, Celtics president and general

Nate Thurmond attempts a hook shot over Dave Cowens as Jo Jo White watches during Game 4 of the Eastern Conference Championship Series, May 14, 1976. (The Cleveland Press Collection, Michael Schwartz Library, Cleveland State University)

manager Red Auerbach raced to the bench when Boston head coach Tom Heinsohn was ejected and immediately inserted Havlicek into the game. "Hondo" failed to score from the field, but he was the inspirational lift his team needed. He did sink two free throws with 11 seconds left to send the Celtics to a 99–94 victory, although the Cavs had pulled within one point with 14 seconds to go. Cowens scored a game-high 26 points. Cleamons led the Cavs with 18. Boston was up three games to two.

Cavaliers players, fans, and media covering the team were more than a little perturbed with the officiating in Game 5. To this day, Thurmond believes something fishy was in the air on that Sunday afternoon in the Garden.

"They cheated us out of that game," he said. "They fouled me out on a clean block on Cowens. There was no contact at all. It wasn't even close. We had 'em. CBS didn't want Cleveland in the championship round. The NBA TV ratings were important. They still are. The networks were worried that it would be us and Phoenix in the Finals."

The Suns wound up shocking defending champion—and heavy favorite—Golden State in Game 7 of the Western Conference Finals later that same day on which the Cavaliers fell to Boston in Game 5.

Thurmond is convinced there was foul play—no pun intended.

"To have Cleveland and Phoenix? Oh-h-h-h, come on! There was no way they wanted that!" he declared. "At least that's what it looked like to me."

"That's always been the urban legend," Sheldon Ocker said, "that CBS didn't want a Cleveland-Phoenix championship series, that the NBA tries to get the matchups it wants and that's how they do it—by the referees' calls. I don't know if that's true or not, but the Cavs totally got hosed in that Game 5 in Boston. For a while I thought, 'Maybe it's just me because I cover the Cavaliers,' but the more I thought about it . . . and I don't know if it was bad refereeing or on purpose . . . it was a pivotal game of the series, and call after call after call went against the Cavaliers, and they were bad calls."

Peticca agreed wholeheartedly.

"The refs didn't let Thurmond, and Brewer, too, do what Cowens and Silas were allowed to do," he said. "That might sound like a fan's typical sour grapes but that still bothers me. Cowens fouled out of Game 2, but for him to get six fouls in the Boston Garden he probably had to commit a dozen."

"Let's face it," Joe Tait said. "The league has, over the years, kind of shaded things one way or another because of television. Television was just starting to rear its ugly head back in the mid-'70s, and obviously they

A choked-up Bill Fitch (*left*) and Nick Mileti prior to Fitch's Coach of the Year trophy presentation before Game 6 of the Eastern Conference Finals, May 18, 1976. (The Cleveland Press Collection, Michael Schwartz Library, Cleveland State University)

wanted to have the best possible draw for TV. I think Cleveland-Phoenix would've been a tremendous series, and it turned out that Boston-Phoenix was a tremendous series. I'm not going to say the TV people went to the officials and said, 'We want Boston to win,' but you sometimes wonder whether or not things happen that at least give the scenario that they want something to occur."

Two nights later, on May 18, another huge crowd, 21,564 once again waited for their heroes to tie the series and send it back to Beantown for a deciding seventh game. Jim Lessig, the color analyst on Cavaliers local television broadcasts in the early- to mid-1970s, will never forget the chills he felt prior to the start of Game 6.

"Gib Shanley, the play-by-play man, and I had done some of the Cavs' postseason games that season," he said, "maybe even a home game or two. We opened the broadcast from down on the floor right in the center jump circle. And when Bill Fitch came down the runway about a minute before the game and that crowd started to cheer, I'd never heard anything like it in my life! Gib turned to me and said, 'Jim, you were here when this all started when we used to draw 3,600 at the old arena downtown. How do you feel right now?' I opened my mouth and nothing came out. I was never at a loss for words as a color man but I was at that moment.

I just choked up. I couldn't believe what I was seeing and hearing after what we started five years earlier."

Once again, it was tight from start to finish. Boston was up 22–19 after one quarter. The Cavs led 46–43 at halftime. The home team reeled off eight straight points to forge ahead 69–61 late in the third quarter. The Celtics pulled to within 69–67 after three. The game was tied at 69, then at 76, and again at 78. A three-point play by Thurmond gave the Cavaliers an 81–78 advantage. A Cowens tip-in put Boston on top, 82–81. A jumper from the circle by Carr, who led Cleveland with 26 points, gave the Cavs an 83–82 lead. White hit a long bomb to put the Celtics up 84–83 with three minutes to go. Russell retaliated with a long bomb of his own, a 25-footer, for an 85–84 Cavs lead. A Brewer steal from Cowens was followed by another 25-foot try by Russell, but this time he missed. White, who scored a game-high 29 points, hit another from downtown for an 86–85 Celtics lead. Scott then stole the ball and drove for a layup. That was it. The bubble was burst. The Cavs lost 94–87. The season was over.

"The crowd gave us a standing ovation," Thurmond recalled. "They realized what we tried to do without Chones."

"Everybody knew they'd seen a team give everything it had short-handed as they were," said Tait.

"We just didn't have the balance we needed," said Cleamons. "But at the end of the day the Celtics won the NBA title, so you've got to take your hat off to them. I certainly do."

Thurmond was crushed.

"We'd gotten bounced on a bad call in a pivotal game [Game 5]," he said. "And after Game 6 was over, I knew that might've been my last shot at a title. Everybody wants to win a ring. Everybody! And at that time I knew how special it was to get that far. Unlike my rookie year, realization had set in: 'Hey, it's hard to get there!'"

"Nate had to go up against Dave Cowens, who was in his prime," Tait said. "He gave it everything he had, but he didn't have the kind of youth in him anymore that he needed."

"Our prayers got answered when Chones went down, although playing against Nate Thurmond was no picnic," Cowens said. "The real issue was that they didn't have two [legitimate] centers for that series. There's a big difference between Jim Chones and Luke Witte. Having Chones out eliminated one of their weapons. Chones was a different player than Thurmond. Chones was more of a physical guy who liked to get inside and rock and roll, and that was a problem for me because he was a lot like me. That's always the toughest guy to play against, somebody who's like you. Nate was just smooth and talented.

"That was the first time I ever played against Nate in a series because he was always in the West playing for the Warriors and then the Bulls. Nate had me bottled up because he was so long that he could back off of you and still bother your jump shot. And so then it was harder to get around him because he was already a little bit further off of you. So he was a really tough guy to figure out. Then in one game I finally started getting something going, but it was really a struggle for me to play against him. He was a heck of an offensive player as well."

"I have no complaints about Nate's performance in that series," Fitch said.

As for Witte's effort, the coach said he could not have asked for more. "Luke was respectable when he played and gave us a chance," he said.

Peticca recalled covering Cleveland Indians games for the Associated Press at old Municipal Stadium at the same time that Cleveland AP sports editor Mike Harris was covering games 3 and 6.

"The attendance figures for those two Tribe games—against Boston first and then New York—were less than 4,000," he said. "They were the smallest crowds for those respective series."

Not only that, but those two crowds—3,832 on May 11 and 3,895 on May 18—were the fifth- and sixth-lowest Indians home crowds for the entire season.

"I would think the Cavs playing at home those nights had some impact on the small crowds," Peticca said.

Peticca also recalled that the scribes covering the Tribe games those two nights were much more interested in what was going on down in Richfield.

"We had a little television that hung from the ceiling of the press box," he said. "I'll never forget during the game against the Red Sox everybody in the press box often crowded around the TV to watch the Cavs-Celtics game, especially during critical moments. And, of course, it was a very close game. Then during the game against the Yankees the Cavs game wasn't televised, at least not in the press box, so I brought a transistor radio—a pretty powerful one. And, especially during the last few minutes of the game, all the guys in the press box crowded around the radio. I also remember that both nights some fans inside the Stadium had radios and that there was a little bit of a buzz when something good happened during the Cavs games."

The prevailing opinion was that, had Chones not been injured, the Cavaliers would have beaten the Celtics and then in the Finals taken care of Phoenix, which won just 42 games during the regular season.

"I certainly feel we would've beaten Boston," said Fitch. "Auerbach talked about that often over the years. He said he was glad he didn't have to sit through that series with Chones playing. We had a few good games against the

Celtics during the regular season and had confidence. I think that would've been a heck of a series. And I don't think there's any doubt that everybody felt whoever won the East that year was going to win the championship."

Ocker agreed wholeheartedly. "The Cavs were the best team in the league," he said. "If Chones hadn't broken his foot, they'd have beaten Boston and would've beaten Phoenix easily. The Suns weren't that good. They would've won it all."

"As you get deeper into the playoffs your bench becomes more and more important," Thurmond said. "And we had that. And we had it in a rotation that was just as smooth as melted butter. And I think, had we been able to knock off Boston, even without Chones we'd have easily beaten Phoenix. With our crowds like they were, [Suns rookie starting center] Alvan Adams wouldn't have wanted to see me."

Peticca, however, isn't so sure that the Cavs would have defeated the Celtics had Chones not been injured. "Their chances would've been better, that's for sure," he said. "And if they'd beaten Boston, you've got to believe they'd have had the upper hand against Phoenix."

Les Levine agreed but put a different spin on it.

"One would've thought," he said, "that the Cavs would've indeed beaten Boston with Chones and then beaten Phoenix. However, you don't know how much was taken out of them by winning that Washington series. Before Chones's injury I think the fan in me was saying, 'It'd be great if we won, but as a guy who sort of understood what the league was all about, I just assumed Boston was going to somehow find a way to win. I didn't think it'd be handed to them with a broken foot, but even *before* the broken foot if I'd had to put a wager on it I probably would've said Boston would win. And, once the injury happened, I think most knowledgeable fans knew that it was going to take a second miracle to beat Boston."

"I didn't understand the magnitude of my injury until 10–15 years later," Chones said, "when I realized that the '76 team had still come the closest of any Cavs team to winning a championship."

Despite falling short of the Finals, the Cavaliers, Mike Snyder believed, hurtled their way into the hearts of Cleveland fans.

"It'd used to be that fans would show up when Wilt Chamberlain or Kareem would come to town," he said, "but beyond that the home games didn't matter much. After the whole experience of the '76 playoffs, though, from that point on the Cavs became one of the big three teams in town."

THE
AFTERMATH

10 | Nick Mileti's Later Years

By 1972 Nick Mileti owned an arena, a basketball team, a baseball team, two hockey teams, and two radio stations. Like the Cavaliers, the Crusaders played their home games at the Cleveland Arena until The Coliseum was built.

"A lot of people had been crazy about the Barons through the years," Bob Dolgan said, "but once Mileti created this newer team, the Crusaders . . . they had bigger names, including former Boston Bruins great Gerry Cheevers, than the Barons, and people started not paying as much attention to the Barons."

The Barons relocated to Jacksonville, Florida, in February 1973. With the Crusaders, for the most part, becoming less competitive as the years went on, Mileti sold them in 1975 to a gentleman by the name of Jay Moore but bought them back from Moore the very next year. With the new NHL Barons coming to town from Oakland, where they were known as the California Golden Seals, Mileti moved the Crusaders to St. Paul, where they became the Minnesota Fighting Saints. He had sold his interest in the Indians to Ted Bonda and other investors in 1975.

"For the most part," said Bill Nichols, "we didn't have good teams in Cleveland in those days, in the '60s and '70s, but Nick made it fun, kind of like Bill Veeck did with the Indians years before but on a smaller scale." One of Mileti's favorite hangouts was the Theatrical Grill downtown.

"The Theatrical Grill was a great restaurant," Dolgan said, "a mecca for the sporting crowd—ballplayers, sportswriters, gamblers, and also lawyers and beautiful girls. The food was superb and the entertainment outstanding. Mileti was a regular there when he was the biggest man in sports in

Cleveland. A lot of people do not have a favorable opinion of Mileti, but I happen to think he was a breath of fresh air. He did a lot for the Cleveland sports scene."

"Nick had to do it sometimes with smoke and mirrors," Joe Tait said, "because he was using a lot of other peoples' money to stay alive when things weren't going that well. But in a very short period of time he amassed the Arena, the Barons, the Cavaliers, 3WE, the FM station, the Indians, the Crusaders, and The Coliseum. He was kind of like an overnight success."

"Nick Mileti," Bill Fitch said, "was as good an owner as anyone would ever want to work for. He was fantastic, one of the finest men I've ever been around."

According to Tom Melody, Mileti was a very genuine person. "He enjoyed the spotlight, there's no question about it," he said, "but at the same time he was extremely down to earth, sincere . . . a good, good man. Of the people I met over the years in sports, I couldn't put anybody ahead of him as my direct relationship with him was concerned. Anytime I was ever around him, he always made me feel at home."

The Cavs' players also loved Mileti.

"Nick was a great guy," said Jim Chones. "He was a happy-go-lucky guy who loved Cleveland. He also took excellent care of his players. Everybody got paid."

"Nick was always encouraging, too," said Austin Carr.

Mileti in 1977 sold 3WE to the Pacific & Southern Company. It became Gannett Broadcasting, which eventually changed the station's handle to Country 11. Larry Morrow was heartbroken. "The new format," he said, "couldn't have lasted more than a year before it switched back to the old one. I had 10 wonderful years there, though, and loved every minute of it."

There were more changes in the 1980 offseason. Mileti sold his 37 percent interest in the Cavaliers to a gentleman by the name of Lou Mitchell, who was on the team's board of directors. When Mitchell realized there was a negative cash flow, he granted a 30-day option to Mileti's cousin Joe Zingale to buy the 37 percent stock for $1 million. Zingale exercised the option and sold the 37 percent interest for $2 million to Nationwide Advertising Service owner Ted Stepien.

"As for The Coliseum," Morrow said, "it wasn't making a lot of money by then and neither were the Cavs. To my understanding, Nick couldn't make the payments to the bank and they decided to pull the plug and take The Coliseum."

Although much of his time and energy in Cleveland were spent on his entrepreneurial ventures, Mileti was also community driven. He started the Cuyahoga Valley Scenic Railroad, with real steam engines, and was on the board of trustees of the Cleveland Metroparks Zoo.

In his last stab at owning a sports franchise, Mileti founded, and was the principal owner of, the short-lived Canadian Football League team, the Las Vegas Posse, in 1994.

Mileti is the author of three books: *Closet Italians: A Dazzling Collection of Illustrious Italians with Non-Italian Names* (2004); *Beyond Michelangelo: The Deadly Rivalry Between Borromini and Bernini* (2005); and *The Unscrupulous: Scams, Cons, Fakes, and Frauds That Poison the Fine Arts* (2009).

Mileti and his wife Bernadette live in Palm Beach, Florida. They travel all over the world; Italy and London are two of their favorite spots. Although he has lived in places such as Rome, New York, and Las Vegas, Mileti, who follows the NBA very little these days, will always have a soft spot for Cleveland. In fact, Nick and Bernadette visit Cleveland a few times a year to spend time with Nick's son Jim from a previous marriage.

Of all of Mileti's endeavors, the one that Cleveland sports fans just might be most thankful for was his purchase of the Indians.

"Nick saved the Indians from moving to New Orleans," Dolgan said. "They'd been contracted to play, I believe, 30 games a year there. There was an actual agreement. And nobody in Cleveland expressed any outrage because the team was losing all the time. I remember writing a couple of columns saying that something had changed, that nobody cared, that nobody got mad when it was announced that the Indians were going to play 30 games a year in New Orleans. One columnist wrote, 'It would be a good idea! They're not drawing too well here. They'll draw a lot better in New Orleans and they'll make more money.' Well, when Mileti heard about the agreement and then read that column, he was outraged. The Indians were for sale so he bought the team and when he did he said, 'The Indians will not be playing any games in New Orleans.' I remember when he came back from the Winter Meetings, that night he walked into the Theatrical Grill and arrived like a conquering hero.

"Frankly, I'm surprised at how much ill feeling there is from some people in Cleveland about Mileti, people who say he was a phony, that he used other people's money to buy ball clubs. Most people do that. There are very few people around who have the cash to simply plunk down all their own money to buy a team. When Art Modell bought the Browns, for example, he and a partner named Rudy Schaefer rounded up their own investors. Nick tried hard to keep Cleveland a big-league town and is a very important man in the city's sports history."

"Nick Mileti," Morrow said, "may have been short in stature, maybe 5-foot-4 or 5-foot-5 tops, but, boy, he had the greatest smile and the most wonderful personality. And when he'd sit down and say, 'Larry, this is my dream, this is what I want to do,' you just bought into it. He was a great leader. A leader is a person who has the ability to have a whole group of people line up behind them for one common purpose based on trust, integrity, humility, and the incredible desire to win for them.

"That was Nick Mileti."

11 | Nothing Lasts Forever, but This Is Ridiculous

The Cavaliers began the 1976–77 season exactly where they left off in 1975–76. With Jim Chones fully healed and basically the same cast of characters as the year before, they reeled off eight wins to start the season and won 16 of their first 20 games. They leveled off somewhat and were 27–22 when Nate Thurmond suffered a left knee injury that, for all intents and purposes, ended his career. With 7-foot, 250-pound Elmore Smith, who had arrived by way of a trade with Milwaukee three-and-a-half weeks earlier, helping out underneath, the Cavs finished 43–39, good enough for the final seed in the now six-team Eastern Conference playoff field. Leading the way were Campy Russell with 16.5 points per game and Austin Carr with 16.2.

Cleveland's best-of-three games first-round playoff opponent? None other than the Washington Bullets, the Cavs' victim in that memorable seven-game playoff series the year before. This series certainly lacked the excitement of the previous season's encounter. The Cavs lost Game 1 in Landover 109–100; they won Game 2 at The Coliseum 91–83, led by Russell's 22 points; but they lost the Game 3 rubber match at Landover 104–98 in a game not nearly as close as the score indicates.

With Jim Cleamons gone, having signed with New York as a free agent, and replaced as compensation by former Knicks great Walt Frazier, the Cavaliers started strong in 1977–78 but then dropped off and struggled to stay above the .500 mark for the majority of the season. A hot finish—nine wins in their last 10 games—resulted in another 43–39 finish and pushed the Cavs into the playoffs as the fourth seed. They were quickly vanquished in the opening round, however, by the Knicks two games to none, getting blown out at home 132–114 in Game 1 and falling 109–107 in Game 2 at Madison Square Garden on Spencer Haywood's jumper from the top of the key with two seconds remaining, wasting a 32-point effort from Russell, who was in his first season as a starter.

"I think maybe the reason the Cavaliers weren't able to sustain the success they had in 1975–76," said Mike Peticca, "was because so much of their excellence in that '75–76 season depended on chemistry. Maybe it was a little fragile, the possibility of maintaining that for much longer. And I think a couple of players started to get a little bit beyond their prime like Dick Snyder, who'd been a terrific player in his first two seasons with the Cavs. And maybe a couple guys, like Jim Brewer, began to go in decline even somewhat prematurely."

"I don't want to say the '75–76 season was a fluke," Les Levine said, "but I just think it was the perfect storm how everything came together that year and for that one series against Washington. Whatever problems they had as a team, whatever weaknesses they had, probably were exposed in the seasons after."

With Snyder, a free agent, off to his former stomping grounds of Seattle and the team a year older, the Cavaliers began the 1978–79 season 4–0 but then lost 14 of their next 15 games. They heated up a little and, after a 112–108 win over Golden State on January 7, their record stood at 17–22. That was the closest they would come to .500 for the rest of the season, a year in which Brewer was traded to the Pistons in February. The Cavs wound up 30–52 and in fifth place in the Central Division. One bright spot was Russell, who averaged a team-high and career-best 21.9 points per game and was the club's lone All-Star. Another was '78 first-round draft pick Mike Mitchell, who averaged almost 11 points per game and would be the team's leading scorer for each of the next two seasons, with a career-best of 24.5 in his lone All-Star campaign of 1980–81.

That '78–79 season was Bill Fitch's last as head coach of the Cavaliers. He resigned on May 21 and took the same position with the Boston Celtics.

"There were a lot of things written that weren't true when I resigned," said Fitch. "I didn't leave because I was going to Boston or anything like that. I left because it was time to go, time to move on. They needed new blood. Nick [Mileti] and I were still getting along, but everybody figured that he and I had a big split and that's why I left, but that wasn't true. Hell, if you go way back, Nick and I had arguments the first year I was there, in probably the first five minutes we were together. But I loved the guy. He was one of a kind. He did a lot of good things for Cleveland. I certainly didn't leave because of Nick Mileti. I left one friend and joined another, Red Auerbach. The reason I went to Boston was out of friendship to Red.

"My dad had died, I'd gone through a divorce, and my mom was 85 years

Bill Fitch at a press conference announcing his resignation as Cavs head coach with Nick Mileti in the rear, May 21, 1979. (Courtesy of AndersonsClevelandDesign.com)

old. She lived to be 100. I'd planned on going home to take care of her, to get things straightened out. I also thought about going back to coach college ball. But, in the meantime, Red had tried to get Bobby Knight and a couple of other guys to coach the Celtics, who'd fallen on hard times. Red wasn't the hard-nosed, bad boss whom everybody said he was. He had a heart of gold. He said to me, 'Bill, would you please come and just take it for a year?' The team had won just 29 games the year before, and that's sacrilegious in Boston."

Fitch was not the only high-profile basketball personality to arrive in Beantown that off-season. Larry Bird flew into town, too. The two of them led the Celtics to a 61–21 record in 1979–80. The team lost to the 76ers in the Eastern Conference Finals but, with Robert Parish and Kevin McHale aboard, got revenge the next year by beating them in the same round in seven games, recovering from a 3–1 series deficit. The Celtics went on to defeat the Houston Rockets for Fitch's lone NBA Championship. The next season, 1981–82, Fitch and the Celts once again trailed Philly 3–1 in the conference finals and, once again, came back to force a seventh game. This time, though, the Sixers prevailed.

Fitch coached the Celtics for one more season before leaving for Houston in 1983. With "Twin Towers" Akeem Olajuwon and Ralph Sampson leading the way, Fitch and the Rockets advanced to the NBA Finals in 1985–86, falling to Fitch's previous team, the Celtics, four games to two. Fitch also had stints with the New Jersey Nets and Los Angeles Clippers before retiring in 1998 with 944 wins, which rank 10th in NBA history.

Fitch's career winning percentage may be below the .500 mark, but the fact is, at every one of his five stops, perhaps other than Boston due to Bird's presence, he took over rebuilding projects and improved the teams year by year for the most part.

"He ought to be a Hall of Famer," Peticca said. "Anytime he had a decent nucleus of players, he won."

These days, Fitch lives about an hour northwest of Houston on Lake Conroe. He has three grown daughters. The middle one, Lisa, took after Dad and was the women's head basketball coach at Walsh College (now Walsh University) and the University of Akron. As Bill put it, "she lives a nine iron away from me." Fitch has four grandsons and three great-grandchildren. He keeps busy with his two dogs and by playing golf or, as he put it, "a game similar to it." He also keeps up with the NBA big time. In fact, he "coaches" every night.

"I just turn on the TV and I'm undefeated," he laughed. "I even got another championship ring, from the Dallas Mavericks five years ago. I gave Rick Carlisle, their head coach, his first coaching job when I was with the Nets. He had a ring made for me."

As for the post-Fitch Cavaliers, their new head coach was Stan Albeck, who had coached for many years, mostly as an assistant, in the college ranks and in the pros. The number of players on the Cavs' roster who were on the Miracle of Richfield team continued to dwindle. Gone was Chones, who was traded to the Lakers. Bingo Smith lasted little more than two weeks into the 1979–80 season before he was traded to the San Diego Clippers.

Newcomers via trades in '79–80 included veteran shooting guard Randy Smith, veteran center Dave Robisch, and power forward Kenny Carr; the latter joined the team some two weeks after the season began. Offense was not a problem for Cleveland as it scored by far the most points in team annals and was the third-highest scoring team in the league, also indisputably the best of any Cavaliers team in history. Unfortunately, there were only three clubs worse than the Cavs in points yielded. The team started slowly, losing seven of its first nine games, but recovered and improved to

19–20 by the time 1980 arrived. One-point home defeats to the Sixers and Bucks were the start of what turned out to be a horrid dawn of the new decade. Out of nowhere, though, beginning on March 7, the Cavs ripped off eight straight wins that, led by Smith's 29 points, culminated in a thrilling 109–105 triumph over the Celtics in front of nearly 20,000 fans in a rocking Coliseum; it also pushed them into the playoff picture. They fell just short, most likely due to a season-ending injury to Russell halfway through the schedule, splitting their final four games to finish with a record of 37–45. There was hope, a light at the end of the tunnel, but Ted Stepien would swoop in and quickly darken that tunnel. Stepien took a franchise already with issues and turned it into a circus.

"It all started," said Kent Schneider, Stepien's attorney at the time, "with the day we made the deal to buy Ted's interest in the team. We made the deal with Joe Zingale, and I explained to Ted that, as soon as we told the press that the purchase had been made, they were going to be all over him asking a million questions. I said to him over and over, 'As difficult as it's going to be you have to keep saying, 'I'm just a shareholder, and until such a time when I'm elected to the Cavs' board of directors and I'm approved by the NBA, I have no comment.' I wake up the next morning, I open the paper, and the first thing I see is a headline that says something to the effect of 'Stepien to fire Ron Hrovat as General Manager.' Mileti had signed Hrovat to a three-year contract prior to the '79–80 season! But Ted couldn't restrain himself. He had no authority to do what he did."

Stepien made another mistake by originally hiring hot-headed Bill Musselman to be the Cavaliers' general manager.

"When Stan Albeck heard that Musselman was coming in," Sheldon Ocker recalled, "he immediately decided, 'Well, I can't stay here.'"

"Albeck was pissed," Schneider said. "He knew he'd be looking over his shoulder and that Musselman, who wanted the coaching job, was Ted's guy. Every one of us said to Ted, 'How can you bring Musselman here? He's the most hated coach in Ohio!' He was the head coach of the Minnesota team that beat up Luke Witte of Ohio State."

"All of this was happening right around the NBA Draft," Ocker continued. "So the day of the Draft Albeck comes in, makes the first pick, stands up, and says, 'That's it, I'm done.' Nobody knew what he was talking about. We didn't know if he meant he was done for the day or he was done drafting or what . . . and he leaves. Nobody knew that Stan was actually quitting. Musselman was already in town. He was sitting in the back of the room but I'm sure he hadn't done any research, hadn't done anything. So Albeck's assistant made the picks until the eighth round. I'm not exactly sure how this happened, but Bill Needle, the Cavaliers' PR guy, wound up making the eighth-round pick. Bill Nichols made the pick in the ninth round. I was supposed to make the 10th-round pick, but I was disgusted with the whole thing and I said, 'I pass,' so the Cavs didn't have a 10th-round pick."

Yes, the PR guy and beat writers were making draft picks!

"Unbeknownst to Ted," recalled Ocker, "who said afterward that he'd wanted Albeck to stay, Albeck had flown to San Antonio to take the head-coaching job with the Spurs. So while Ted's praising Stan and saying how he wants him to stay, Albeck's at a press conference in San Antonio saying, 'I'm glad to be with the Spurs.' Albeck was only able to break the contract and do that because he'd gone to Nick Mileti and said, 'You've got to let me out of my contract because Musselman's coming.' So Mileti, with only days left of his ownership of the team, let Albeck out of his contract."

All of the preceding chaos resulted in Musselman becoming the Cavaliers' head coach and Stepien acting as his own general manager. Stepien traded three—yes, three—first-round draft picks to the expansion Dallas Mavericks for guard Mike Bratz, power forward Richard Washington, and center Jerome Whitehead, the latter two some three weeks into the 1980–81 season. Another first-rounder was traded to Dallas for point guard Geoff Huston in early February. Other newcomers included rookie center Bill Laimbeer, who was actually a 1979 Cavs draft choice, and shooting guard Roger Phegley, obtained in a trade with New Jersey.

Another change Stepien made was to the team's uniform. The gold shade was altered from yellowish to metallic, and the checkerboard pattern was removed. Two stripes—white and gold—were placed below a newly fonted "CLEVELAND" and above the uniform number, still the only time in team history in which the city name was featured on both the home and road jerseys. Although unpopular, it wasn't one of Stepien's worst moves, for at least he preserved the wine and gold color scheme.

With Austin Carr gone to Dallas via the Expansion Draft and Foots Walker and Russell traded to the Nets and Knicks, respectively, backup big man John Lambert, Cleveland's first-round draft pick out of the University of Southern California in 1975, was the lone remnant of the Miracle of Richfield team by the time the 1980–81 season arrived. And he was next, waived 10 weeks into the schedule. (Russell would return to the Cavs for the first week-and-a-half of the 1984–85 season.)

The Cavaliers got off to a rough start in '80–81 and were just 12–27 after a 100–98 loss to Chicago on the day after Christmas. Ten wins in their next 15 games, however, improved their record to 22–32 at the All-Star break.

Unfortunately, this is where another of Stepien's embarrassing misadventures came into play. The Cavs were actually set to host their very first All-Star Game on February 1.

"All through that season," Ocker said, "Stepien had put on halftime shows that had Don 'Boots' Buttrey, a guy who opened beer cans with his teeth, set off firecrackers in his mouth, ate doughnuts whole, and all of that kind of stuff. Stepien also had this guy named 'Crazy George' who did all kinds of crazy dribbling. He also had the 'Teddy Bears,' the Cavs' dance team he'd concocted, dancing around, too."

"So at some point before the All-Star Game," recalled Mike Peticca, "a representative for NBA commissioner Larry O'Brien called Joe Tait and asked him to fly to New York and talk with the commissioner. So Joe flew to New York and O'Brien asked Joe, 'What's going on in Cleveland with this owner?'"

Thus, O'Brien was well aware of Stepien and his buffoonery. He could have never imagined, however, what was in store by the time of the kick-off luncheon to the All-Star Game on Friday, January 30.

"Besides O'Brien, who was also the former head of the Democratic Party," said Schneider, "also at the luncheon were David Stern, the NBA's general counsel and future commissioner, and a couple other bigwigs. Ted's offices were in the old Statler Office Tower at East 12th and Euclid, so he has this luncheon at the Statler. And he entertained these people with Buttrey, Crazy George, and the Teddy Bears doing their stuff!"

"From what I heard," laughed Mike Snyder, "they also had a polka band. A polka song had replaced *Come On Cavs* as the team fight song!"

"Think about it," Schneider said. "The commissioner's there at the All-Star luncheon! All the dignitaries are there! It's supposed to be a fairly elegant affair, and Ted has this doughnut-eating guy out there! It was bizarre! I'm sitting there looking up at where O'Brien and Stern are sitting. Stern and I had become good friends because we were in contact so often because the NBA had so many problems dealing with Ted. The next day the league calls Ted and tells him, 'We've taken over control of the All-Star Game. It will remain in Cleveland, but you're out! You have no decision-making authority. You have absolutely nothing to do with the game.' After they saw what Ted did, they were scared to death of what was going to happen if he was in control of putting on the actual All-Star Game."

"They took it out of the Cavs' hands!" declared Peticca. "I think that's still unprecedented."

As for the All-Star Game itself, which went on without a hitch in front of a crowd of 20,239, Mitchell's 14 points not only gave the home fans something

Mike Mitchell, 1980. (Courtesy of AndersonsClevelandDesign.com)

Left to right: Don Delaney, Ted Stepien, and Bill Musselman at a press conference announcing that Delaney would replace Musselman as Cavs head coach for the final 11 games of the season, March 13, 1981. (The Cleveland Press Collection, Michael Schwartz Library, Cleveland State University)

for which to cheer, they also helped the East to a 123–120 triumph over the West. Unfortunately, the Cavaliers came out of the break ice cold, dropping five straight games on the way to a 28–54 final record. New general manager Don Delaney replaced Musselman for the last 11 games.

Joe Tait, for one, couldn't stand Stepien. He'd had enough of his shenanigans and made it abundantly clear during broadcasts. Stepien made it clear through the press that he didn't appreciate Tait's barbs against him. By the late stages of the season, it had become a war of words.

"After the season 3WE gave the Cavs' broadcast rights to Stepien," said Tait, "because they didn't want to be associated with him any longer. The station gave me a settlement for the two years remaining on my contract, and I left after the season."

It was a good thing Tait left, for he could have ended up in jail.

"Had I stayed there beyond the one year," he said, "I would've killed Stepien. He would've fired me anyway. I was going through a divorce at the same time I was dealing with him, and I enjoyed the divorce more."

Before he left, the Cavaliers honored their living legend with "Joe Tait Night" in their final home game of the season on March 27 against Philadelphia. The fact that 20,175 fans showed up for a team that was 24 games below .500 was proof positive that Tait would be missed—big time. The angry crowd used the occasion to not only show support for its adored

With empty seats behind them, Ted Stepien (*left*) and Bill Musselman prior to a home game with Chicago, April 7, 1982. (The Cleveland Press Collection, Michael Schwartz Library, Cleveland State University)

broadcaster, whom Stepien was running out of town, but also voice its discontent over the fact that Stepien was staying behind to run the team.

By the time the 1981–82 season arrived, Stepien's popularity in Cleveland was at an all-time low and the Cavaliers were referred to locally as the "Cadavers." It might seem hard to believe, but the '81–82 season was even worse than the '80–81 campaign. The following is a sample of what 1981–82 brought:

- The Cavs began the season 4–13 under Delaney as head coach.
- Assistant coach Bob Kloppenburg replaced Delaney for just one game, a loss.
- Chuck Daly replaced Kloppenburg and went 9–32.
- Musselman returned to coach the final 23 games, 21 of which he lost.
- Mitchell and Phegley were traded to San Antonio for shooting guard Ron Brewer and power forward Reggie Johnson.
- Less than two months later, Johnson was traded to Kansas City for power forward Cliff Robinson.
- Laimbeer and Carr were traded to Detroit for bumbling center Paul Mokeski.

Perhaps the most memorable of those moves was the one that sent Mitchell and Phegley to the Spurs. Peticca remembered it well.

"It was a home game against Kansas City two days before Christmas," he said, "and I believe it was halftime. Stepien tells us—the media—in the media room about the trade. We, the reporters, go into the locker room after the game and tell Mitchell he's been traded! He hadn't even been told! That's how things were being run!"

Twenty-three players suited up for the Cavaliers in 1981–82, a season that ended with 19 straight losses and a 15–67 record. The soap opera continued in 1982–83 when the team lost its first five games for an NBA-record, at the time, 24 straight defeats dating back to the previous season. Veteran NBA and ABA head coach Tom Nissalke replaced Musselman that year and actually lasted two full seasons. A month-and-a-half into the schedule Brewer was shipped to Golden State for shooting guard World B. Free, a trade, finally, that benefited the team, a move that was actually orchestrated by a bright, young president, and soon-to-be general manager, named Harry Weltman, whom Stepien had recently hired at Schneider's urging. Free's long bombs were about all that Cavs fans had to cheer in a 23–59 season. Attendance at The Coliseum had dropped every year but one since it peaked at 13,913 per game in 1976–77:

- 11,097 in 1977–78
- 7,942 in 1978–79
- 7,873 in 1979–80
- 5,475 in 1980–81
- 5,769 in 1981–82
- 3,916 in 1982–83

"It was something to see," said Schneider. "When Ted made the decision, for instance, initially to bring Musselman in, I thought it was a horrible decision. When he hired Delaney to be the GM and eventually the head coach . . .

this guy had been the head coach at Lakeland Community College and Dyke College [now Chancellor University] during the previous decade or so!"

Then there was the infamous "Bagley-Magley" draft in 1982. As Levine explained: "I was told that Stepien actually drafted David Magley because it rhymed with John Bagley, who was drafted one round before him, that he thought it was cute."

"Stepien has got to be the worst owner in the history of professional sports," said Tom Hardesty. "It was a situation where the ownership just destroyed morale. No one knew how long anybody was going to be around. The team may have had some talent individually, but there was no continuity or stability. The real Miracle of Richfield was that the Cavaliers survived the Stepien era and remained in Northeast Ohio!"

"Stepien got the worst media treatment of any person I ever saw in Cleveland," Bob Dolgan said. "There was a writer who deliberately misspelled his name every time he mentioned him in his column."

As for all of those first-round draft picks that "Terrible Ted," as he was known to many, traded away, the NBA took notice and acted quickly in devising the "Stepien Rule," which prohibits teams from trading first-round draft picks in consecutive seasons. Stepien finally sold the Cavaliers to a local group headed by brothers George and Gordon Gund. With the help of four—but not free—bonus first-round draft choices that the NBA restored to the team during the next four years, the ever-appreciative Gunds aimed to alleviate the stench that still lingered from the Stepien era. They went a little overboard by overhauling the team colors to a burnt orange, white, and royal blue. They scrapped the team logo, substituting the word "CAVS" in an arched pattern with the letter "V" in the shape of a hoop and a circle above as a basketball. The burnt orange acted as the primary color on the road uniform and the secondary color on the white home uniform. With several more changes to the team's attire and logo on the way, the wine and gold would not return for 20 years.

Other than changing the Cavaliers' look, the new owners did just about everything right. Still, it took a long time for the franchise to recover from the serious damage Stepien had brought upon it. The team went 28–54 in the Gunds' first season of 1983–84. Back in the fold that year was Tait. After stints as the New Jersey Nets' radio play-by-play man in 1981–82 and the Chicago Bulls' cable television play-by-play man in 1982–83, as well as broadcasting the *CBS Radio College Basketball Game of the Week*, Tait was back where he belonged.

"Harry Weltman called me," said Tait, "and asked if I'd be interested in returning to the Cavaliers. I said, 'Absolutely.'"

Tait's second stint with the Cavs would last much longer than his first.

He stuck around through the 2010–11 season, after which he was replaced by John Michael and Jim Chones. In 1987 he was named the team's vice president of broadcast services, a position that he held until his retirement. On March 26, 2008, Tait announced his 3,000th game for the Cavaliers, against the New Orleans Hornets. The radio broadcast location at Quicken Loans Arena, in section C126, has been forever renamed "The Joe Tait Perch" in honor of that achievement.

During the 2010–11 preseason Tait was hospitalized with pneumonia, and further testing showed he needed heart surgery. This caused him to miss most of that '10–11 season in which Chones and Mike Snyder replaced him on an interim basis. Tait returned to call the Cavs' final dozen games of the season. On April 8, in a game against Chicago, the team honored Tait with "Joe Tait Appreciation Night" and by raising a commemorative banner with his name, his years as a Cavaliers broadcaster, and a microphone next to the Cavaliers retired numbers. Tait's final game was the April 13 contest between the Cavs and Washington Wizards. The Cavs sent him out a winner, defeating Washington 100–93. As the final minute played out, Frank Sinatra's "My Way" blared throughout The Q as cameras focused on his final call as a Cavs broadcaster. Tait's health issues were not the only factor that hastened his retirement.

"The other thing," he said, "was the business of promotion, game presentation, and all of that stuff that really started to overshadow the game of basketball, things like the screaming idiots who come out on the floor and dance around like half-wits. I hated that. One of my favorite stories is after I'd gone to work for the Cavaliers on a full-time basis in 1987, we were having a meeting of the franchise's hierarchy. They were talking about possibly doing pregame shows, halftime shows, and all kinds of stuff like that and I said, 'You know, the Boston Celtics have the best presentation in the league.' And they all said, 'What do they do? What do they do?' And I said, 'They roll the ball rack out on to the center of the floor at halftime and let everybody go take a pee and buy more popcorn.' And they said, 'Well, what does that get you?' And I said, 'They also happen to win 60 games a year.' But now everybody, even the Celtics, has got a mascot, dancing girls, and all of that other crap."

Tait's resume also includes four seasons, from 1988 to 1992, of calling Cavs games on television when he wasn't calling them on radio and 15 years as a broadcaster for the Cleveland Indians—seven on radio and eight on television, respectively—from 1973–87.

"Working with Herb Score was really a treat," he said. "We had a good chemistry. Broadcasting baseball was harder than basketball because you had to keep the tempo of the game up even though the game itself had a very sporadic tempo. There were a lot of down times in a broadcast that you had to kind of talk your way through."

Tait had the pleasure of calling three no-hitters—Dick Bosman's against the soon-to-be three-time defending World Series Champion Oakland A's on July 19, 1974; Dennis Eckersley's against the California Angels on May 30, 1977; and Len Barker's perfect game against the Toronto Blue Jays on May 15, 1981.

"Bosman's was probably number one on my hit parade," he said, "because he was a journeyman pitcher at the end of a long career who had his moment of glory."

Tait served as the radio play-by-play voice of the WNBA's Cleveland Rockers from 1997–2003. He has done play-by-play for the Mount Union College Purple Raiders football team on cable TV's *SportsTime Ohio* since 2008. He is on Mount Union's board of trustees. He also calls high school basketball games for WEOL-AM 930 in Elyria. In 2011 Tait co-authored his memoir, *Joe Tait—It's Been a Real Ball,* with sportswriter Terry Pluto. The following are Tait's awards and honors:

- Eight-time National Sportscasters and Sportswriters Association Ohio Sportscaster of the Year (1974, 1976, 1978, 1991, 1996, 1999, 2002, 2003)
- Ohio Broadcasters Hall of Fame inductee (1992)
- Cleveland Association of Broadcasters Hall of Fame inductee (1997)
- Cleveland Press Club Journalism Hall of Fame inductee (2003)
- Indiana Broadcasters Hall of Fame inductee (2004, founding member)
- Greater Cleveland Sports Hall of Fame inductee (2005)
- 2010 Basketball Hall of Fame Curt Gowdy Media Award
- 2012 Ohio Athletic Conference Bill Nichols Media Award

Tait and his wife Jean have been married for 35 years. They live in Lafayette Township in Medina County. Tait has three grown children from a previous marriage, Christina, Karen, and Joe, and two grandchildren.

"In fact," he said, "Karen ran camera for both Cavs and Indians home games for a number of years."

As for hobbies, Tait is a huge fan of railroads.

"I've got about eight model railroad tracks down in the basement," he said. "Maybe someday I'll be able to get one or two of them cooking. The most I do now is break out a train and put it around the base of the Christmas tree. I ride trains anytime I get a chance. Herb Score and I used to ride them from Baltimore up to New York and New York to Boston. Whenever the schedule allowed us to, we took the train. Years ago, Jeannie and I took the train from Cleveland to Chicago and Chicago to Las Vegas. I've ridden the Cuyahoga Valley line numerous times and various other excursions that have come to pass around the area."

World B. Free in action against the Bucks. (Courtesy of AndersonsClevelandDesign.com)

Fans may be surprised to learn that, other than the night of March 4, 2016, when the Miracle of Richfield team was honored, Tait has not seen a single Cavs game—in person or on television—since he retired.

"I'm just not interested," he said. "I'm done. If you're a postman and you've walked your route for 30 years and you retire, what's the first thing you're gonna do on the first day of retirement? It sure isn't taking another long walk! I have nothing but the best possible hopes, though, for the Cavaliers to win it all, I really do. It'd be great for the fans and certainly the city."

Those same fans will never forget Tait's game broadcasts throughout almost 40 wonderful years that included his signature calls such as:

- "It's basketball time at The Coliseum!"
- "Wham with a right/left hand!"
- "To the line, to the lane . . ."
- "Sights it, shoots it, got it."
- "It's a standing 'O-o-o-o' for the guys in go-o-o-old!"
- "Have a good night, ev-v-v-verybody!"

Not only had Tait returned to the Cavaliers in 1983–84, so had 3WE. After two seasons on WBBG-AM 1260 with former Cavs public address announcer

Paul Porter calling the action, the team's game broadcasts were back on 1100. Things in Cavs Land were slowly returning to normal.

George Karl replaced Nissalke in 1984–85, a season that saw the Cavaliers start 2–19 but, led by Free and a surprisingly effective supporting cast, recover remarkably, enough for a 36–46 record and the final seed in the now eight-team Eastern Conference Playoffs, the franchise's first postseason berth in seven years. Karl's squad put up a gallant effort against Bird and Boston in the first round, losing three games to one in an extremely competitive series. The Cavs won just 29 games under Karl and Gene Littles in 1985–86. Former NBA great Wayne Embry took over as general manager after that season. Embry hired none other than Lenny Wilkens as head coach and made many fine moves—including a sensational 1986 Draft day that brought to town Brad Daugherty, Ron Harper, and Mark Price, the latter by way of a deal with Dallas—that built the team into a contender for several years. The Cavs, however, simply couldn't pass the Michael Jordan test. With Mike Fratello as their new head coach in 1993–94 and Gund Arena (now "The Q") as their new downtown digs in 1994–95, the team leveled off somewhat. It wasn't bad but got nowhere in the playoffs.

The late-1990s and early 2000s brought coaching changes galore and poor records, the low point coming in 2002–03 when the Cavaliers finished 17–65, tied for the worst mark in the league. That dreadful '02–03 season, however, resulted in the team winning that spring's NBA Draft Lottery, which brought the one and only LeBron James to the shores of Lake Erie from his home just down I-77 in Akron. The Cavs soon became title contenders—including a Finals appearance in 2007—until LeBron's infamous "Decision" in 2010, which had him flying south for the winters to Miami. "King James" returned to the North Coast in 2014, restoring hope to Cavs fans, including another Finals berth in 2015, that the franchise will soon bring to Cleveland something that not even the Miracle of Richfield team could—a parade down Euclid Avenue.

THE
WINE
AND
GOLD

12 | Jim Cleamons

Jim Cleamons was the ultimate student of the game of basketball. He was like a sponge, soaking up everything he could wherever he was. Take his rookie season in the NBA when he was a member of the 1971–72 World Champion Los Angeles Lakers. He was like a kid in a candy store, for he had future Hall of Famers Jerry West, Gail Goodrich, Elgin Baylor, and Wilt Chamberlain from whom to learn.

"I'd talk to them, and my other teammates, as much as I could every day in practice, after practice, and during every game, learning as much as I could," said Cleamons, who later would play for the Cavaliers. "I was the only rookie who made the team that year. Those guys were like my big brothers. They'd tell me the things I needed to do, about the different players I'd be competing against, what this guy or that guy liked to do . . . it was a wonderful learning experience that season."

Learning was nothing new to Cleamons. He basically taught himself how to play basketball as a young boy growing up in Columbus. He played baseball and football, too, and he was actually best at the former.

"People used to say, 'This kid's gonna have a Major League Baseball career,'" he said. "Willie Mays was one of my idols, but I was a Dodger fan because of Jackie Robinson, Roy Campanella, Don Newcombe, and that bunch. I was an outfielder, mainly in center. I had a nice little arm on me, and as I began to grow, and being left-handed, pitching became one of my favorite positions."

Basketball, however, won out because of its easy access.

"In baseball," Cleamons said, "you need somebody to play catch with. In football you need someone to throw the ball to you. But in basketball

all you need is the hoop and the ball. You could practice your shooting and you could develop your dribbling skills on the way to the playground or while you were at the playground trying to create a shot for yourself. So basketball kind of became my friend and companion because I didn't need anyone else but the ball and the hoop for company. And I realized that the more time I spent working on those things—shooting and dribbling—I was getting to be halfway decent at them."

Cleamons was born on September 13, 1949, in the tiny town of Lincolnton, North Carolina. His parents divorced when he was very young. His mother moved to the Detroit suburb of Bloomfield Hills to be a housekeeper and nanny for a family there. Cleamons lived with some aunts before he, along with some uncles and siblings, moved to Columbus, just before he entered the third grade, to live with his mother, who had relocated from Michigan.

"We had a full house," he laughed.

By the time Cleamons was in the seventh grade, he had taught himself the basics of basketball well enough that he could start competing against other boys.

"About that time," he said, "we moved and put a hoop on the garage behind the house in an alley. It became a hangout, a gathering place, for those of us who lived between the streets and the alley. So even when I wasn't back there playing, the neighborhood kids would come and play."

Logistics kept Cleamons from playing organized basketball until the ninth grade, but he continued competing on the playgrounds, honing his skills. The fact that he had to wait until grade nine to play organized ball was good timing, for that is when he really started to grow.

"I played what was called Hi-Y Basketball," he said. "It was affiliated with the local YMCA and was a program for those who weren't good enough to play varsity junior high school basketball. I was a starter from the second game on. The coach told me one thing. He said, Get the ball moving. We didn't necessarily have a point guard, we just had two guards and my assignment was to get the ball moving. If you want to equate it to what a point guard is today, that'd be a pretty fair comparison. I brought the ball up the court. I ended up being the leading scorer, averaging 10 or so points per game. We won the championship, and it was all by sheer coming together and enjoying each other's company.

"That was the start of my basketball career." And what a career it would turn out to be.

Cleamons attended Linden-McKinley High School. "There were like six middle schools," he said, "that fed into Linden-McKinley and I was a guy who wasn't even good enough to play on one of those junior high schools' varsity teams. There was no way in the world that I was thinking I was good enough to make the reserve team as a sophomore."

But he did. And he started.

"We lost the very first game we played by one point and then won the rest of the games in about a 15-game schedule," he said. "It was the first time in Linden-McKinley's history that the reserves competed like that. Even though I didn't play any varsity minutes, the coach let me dress for varsity games. It gave me an opportunity to see the culture of what was in store for me if I kept working hard. I also got a chance to scrimmage more with the varsity. It was good grooming."

On top of that, Cleamons had a terrific attitude.

"There was no shortage of my desire to compete regardless of the sport," he said. "I always tried to be coachable, too. I realized, in sports, it was important to be able to understand and follow directions and to hold myself accountable to be a good teammate, to be someone who was deserving to be on the team and who was willing to do whatever he could to contribute to the success of the team."

By his junior year Cleamons was a starter on the varsity squad.

"I was no longer a guard, I was a forward," he said. "We were a small team. I was 6-foot-2 at that point. I was also a second-string guard and a third-string center and virtually played the entire game unless it was a blowout. My learning curve was now accelerated because I was in uncharted territory in terms of basketball. If I was going to play all three positions I had to know how to be successful, I had to learn the mechanics of the game, the nuances of the game, what a guard did, what a forward did, what a center did. It wasn't good enough just to play the positions. I actually learned how to master the positions. I felt I did a good job at that. My eyes became fixated on precision, on execution, on excellence. There was no telling at what point in the game I might have to play that position.

"I grew up with people who were as competitive as I was, but they wanted to just play. I not only wanted to play, I wanted to learn, so it became my mission as an athlete to learn how to master the game of basketball if I was going to play it. And by my junior year my goal was, both as an athlete and intellectual in how this game was played, being fulfilled and stimulated because it became intriguing to me, how to win, what was important to win, how important it was to compete. I loved winning, but winning was not an obsession. How to get the most out of my ability and being a good player was. This helped me understand my coach, who was an excellent coach. The little things, the finer points, became very important because that's what made his basketball teams winners. You can win a game by playing sloppily, but if you become fixated on the finer points in the game you can be very successful. You have to work with four people in harmony with some type of chemistry."

Cleamons received a full scholarship in 1967 to play for Fred Taylor at Ohio State University. At that point, a professional basketball career was the furthest thing from his mind.

"There are thousands of kids across the country," he said, "who've been told their whole lives how good they are and that the world is their oyster, so to speak, and they're just biding their time to show people the skills and talent they have. I wasn't of that ilk. I wasn't even All-State in high school, so why would I think I was going to be a professional basketball player? I'd have been a fool! But I'm a competitor and I'm a student of the game, and I just kept learning and improving."

By the time he got to OSU, Cleamons had the reputation of being cat-quick. "In fact," he said, "the Ohio State radio announcer called me 'The Cougar.'"

After starting at guard on the Buckeyes' freshman team (the NCAA prohibited freshmen from playing on the varsity level until 1972–73), Cleamons was back at guard and, as a sophomore starter in 1968–69, averaged 16.6 points and 7.4 rebounds per game, helping Ohio State to a 17–7 record and a tie for second place in the Big Ten.

"In Fred Taylor's system," he said, "you were happy if you played at all as a sophomore because you earned your rights to minutes, you earned your rights to participate, you earned your rights to be on the team, and as you got up there certain allowances were given to you because you earned the right."

As a junior, Cleamons averaged 21.6 points and eight rebounds per game as OSU finished 17–7 again and in a tie for third in the conference.

"By my senior year," he said, "I was the only one of four seniors who played major minutes, so I had the proverbial green light. You couldn't tell me that I wasn't going to average 25–30 points a game and that I wasn't just gonna kick ass. But we had a sophomore guard by the name of Allan Hornyak who tried to do everything I wanted to do or could do. And I knew right away that that script wasn't going to work because I wanted to win. Allan didn't know a damn thing about winning. I had to teach him how to win. We weren't going to win the Big Ten with two guards on a guard-dominated team. That just wasn't going to happen in those days. You had to have balance. And I was the older person in the equation and I wanted to win, especially because, in those days, if you didn't win your conference you weren't going to the NCAA Tournament. Your ass was going home and you were going to talk about what you could've done, what you should've done, and what you didn't do and that was win. And I wanted to win, so I allowed Allan to be the scorer and I took a role of being a defensive play-er, a playmaker, and lowering my scoring opportunities because I knew it was important to winning, and I didn't want to go out my senior year not winning the Big Ten and not playing in the NCAA tourney.

"I'm not saying that Allan was a selfish player, but Allan was Allan. He was recruited for his offense. He scored 86 points in a game in high school. That's what Allan did. And, as a senior, I wasn't going to change him overnight. So, at some point in time, if you're a true leader you've got to look at your group and say, 'This is what these people do and you've got to try to find a way to win with them.' I didn't have enough time to take Allan to the woodshed after every game and every practice and read him the riot act. You've got to figure out what your team has to do in order to win, and in order for our team to win I had to give Allan more shots than I took at any point in time, find a way to win the game. That's what the important thing was."

Cleamons's plan worked to a T. Led by Hornyak's team-high 22.5 points per game, Cleamons's future Cavs teammate Luke Witte's 18.9 points per contest, and Cleamons's 17.4 points per game, Ohio State finished 20–6 and Big Ten Champions. They almost made it to the Final Four, losing by just three points to Western Kentucky in the Mideast Regional Final after having beaten Marquette by one in a regional semifinal.

Even when he was voted Big Ten MVP and an All-American his senior year, Cleamons still was not convinced that a pro basketball career might lie ahead.

"That all didn't make a difference to me," he said, "because I just trusted in myself that I was going to be a good player and continue to grow and develop. My job was to go play and kick that guy's butt who was in front of me and then let the chips fall where they may. It wasn't my job to say how good I was. Even now, I let the history books decide that."

Needless to say, Cleamons, also an Academic All-American his senior year who majored in education, did not expect to be a first-round selec-tion in the 1971 NBA Draft. But he was. The Lakers chose him with the 13th overall pick.

"I was very happy to be drafted," he said. "I was hopeful, optimistic . . . I mean, who *wouldn't* want to play professional basketball, be a professional athlete in a children's game given the opportunity? The next year the Lakers drafted another point guard, Jim Price from Louisville, because the '71–72 season was supposed to have been West's last, but he decided that he had another year or two left in his tank and stayed. So all of a sudden they had a bunch of guards, and I became expendable. They traded me to the Cavaliers."

Although he was returning to the state in which he was raised, the 6-foot-3, 185-pound Cleamons was crushed.

"The Cavs were one of the worst teams in the league," he said. "Nobody respected them. Here I was, going from a team that'd just won the NBA title to the laughingstock of the league. But you realize that you're a professional, and part of being a professional is accepting what comes in front of you. I'd been a competitor my entire life, so it was just another huge challenge to deal with."

Cleamons's first impression of Bill Fitch?

"I knew Coach Fitch had a military background," he said, "so I saw him as a taskmaster–drill sergeant type of personality. And I knew he'd been a successful coach at his previous stops. In high school I had a great coach, I had a great coach in college, and I'd just won an NBA title with Bill Sharman as head coach, so I felt I had a pretty good background of coaches who'd taught me the game. Like I said before, I always saw myself as a student of the game so I welcomed the opportunity to learn as much basketball as I possibly could. Lenny Wilkens was a wonderful addition to the Cavs that year as a veteran player. He was my mentor and I was his protégé. And I can honestly say that Lenny Wilkens taught me how to become a point guard. I could play the game, but I was not a point guard; I was a guard. I could score even though I wasn't asked to. I relished the fact that I wasn't a 'scorer' but I could score. I could play defense, I could rebound . . . I was an all-around player, a complete player."

Cleamons found himself in a situation not unlike the one he was in with Hornyak during his senior year at Ohio State.

"I knew that, for me to survive as a player and for our franchise to get turned around, I had to assume a role that I wasn't accustomed to," he said. "I was going to have to give up a lot of my game individually for the team's sake, and that meant giving up shots, opportunities, and the ability to score to instead share the ball with other guys because that's the way the team was being developed. And I wanted to win. I wanted to win above all else, so that's what I did. Austin Carr was drafted by Cleveland the year before for one reason—he was a great scorer. That's what Coach Fitch wanted from him. So I backed off a little and let Austin get his points. And that helped our team in the long run."

Cleamons was as unselfish a player as they come.

"Jim could hit the jump shot but he rarely, if ever, looked for his shot first," Dick Snyder said.

"That was just his mentality," said Mike Peticca. "He was very underrated and underappreciated. He was also a terrific defensive player who was pretty big for a point guard in those days."

Jim Cleamons drives to the hoop against the Rockets, February 22, 1976. (The Cleveland Press Collection, Michael Schwartz Library, Cleveland State University)

With Wilkens off to Portland just prior to the 1974–75 season, Cleamons became the starting point guard. With "Clem" as their "quarterback," the Cavs barely missed the playoffs that year, almost advanced to the Finals in the Miracle of Richfield season in which his memorable reverse layup at the buzzer won Game 5 of their opening series against Washington, and qualified for the postseason again in 1976–77. Cleamons was the team leader in assists in each of those three seasons and put up 11.9, 12.2, and 10.4 points per game, respectively, those years.

"Clem knew where everybody should be," Nate Thurmond said. "He didn't make a lot of mistakes with the basketball."

Cleamons left for New York as a free agent and spent two-plus seasons with the Knicks before getting traded to Washington and playing for the Bullets through the end of the 1979–80 season. He then decided to call it quits and took a couple of years off to decide what he wanted to do with his life. It should come as no surprise to anyone that he ventured into the coaching profession, putting his education degree to use, in a sense.

"I'd always said I wanted to teach the game of basketball at the college level," Cleamons said, "and I got an opportunity to go to Furman University as an assistant coach. After a year there, I coached under Eldon Miller at Ohio State for four years."

Cleamons then accepted the head-coaching position at Youngstown State University and stayed there for two seasons. He then went to the pros and coached under Phil Jackson in Chicago through 1996 and was a part of four NBA title teams. Asked what it was like to coach Michael Jordan, Cleamons paused before responding.

"It was pure joy," he said.

After that, Cleamons was hired as head coach of the Dallas Mavericks, with whom he spent a little more than one season. After a short stint as head coach of the Chicago Condors of the women's professional American Basketball League, whose star player was Yolanda Griffith, he returned to coach under Jackson again, this time with the Lakers, and spent five seasons in L.A., winning three more NBA championships. Cleamons took an assistant coaching job with the New Orleans/Oklahoma City Hornets, where he stayed for two seasons, before returning to coach under Jackson, who was back with the Lakers again after a one-year respite, through 2011, winning two more titles. He became the head coach of a professional team in China for a year, then sat out for a season before joining the Milwaukee Bucks' staff in 2013 and the Knicks' staff in 2014.

Cleamons and his wife Cheryl have been married for 21 years. They have two daughters, Imani, 17, and Rose, 15. The family lives outside of White Plains, New York. Cleamons truly loves what he does for a living.

"I enjoy watching people learn and I enjoy what athletics can teach people," he said. "What happens is that people want to win, but in their search of trying to win they don't look at it as a way of learning how to improve themselves as individuals, and they get caught up on the winning track. There's a way to win. Winning is a by-product of all the other things that culminate into that process of good work, good ethics, good character, sacrifice, and all those things that we deem successful. It doesn't just happen. And talent is one thing that is way overrated when it comes to winning. Of course, you need talent but you need the talent to also be of good character and of good heart and soul."

Jim Cleamons started off as a student of the game. He now teaches it. A basketball lifer if there ever was one.

13 | Dick Snyder

When Cavaliers fans think of "The Shot," they cringe as they picture Michael Jordan hitting a straightaway—but off-balance—jumper with no time left to give the Chicago Bulls a 101–100 victory over Cleveland at The Coliseum on May 7, 1989. Jordan's buzzer beater eliminated the Cavs from the first round of the playoffs for the second straight year, both times by the Bulls and each time in a deciding fifth game.

Many Cleveland fans can remember another miraculous shot, one made in the same venue 13 years earlier. This one, however, brings back pleasant memories. On April 29, 1976, the Cavaliers were pitted against the veteran-laden Washington Bullets in the seventh game of what had been a riveting Eastern Conference Semifinal playoff series. The contest was a seesaw battle, and the Cavs and Bullets were tied at 85 with just nine seconds remaining.

One Cavalier who will never forget those final nine seconds is Dick Snyder, a native of North Canton and a three-sport star at Hoover High School in the late 1950s and early '60s. Snyder was responsible for one of the most memorable endings in Cleveland sports history. He banked in a running, one-handed shot from five feet away with four seconds left to give the Cavs a two-point lead and, after the Bullets failed to score on their ensuing possession, an 87–85 victory that, because of the thunderous roar of the crowd, just about brought The Coliseum's roof down. Unfortunately, five days later Jim Chones's broken foot quite possibly kept Snyder and the Cavs from beating Boston in the next round and advancing to the NBA Finals in which they would have opposed a Phoenix team that had won just 42 games during the regular season.

Snyder was born on February 1, 1944. Growing up, he had no idea a professional basketball career lay ahead. In addition to playing hoops for Hoover, Snyder copped All-State honors in two other sports as a senior: he quarterbacked the football team and pitched and played in the outfield in baseball. In fact, Snyder's passion was baseball.

"My dream was to make it to the big leagues someday," he said. "I grew up watching my dad play in different leagues around the area, so I was always around it."

Snyder, however, was most sought after by college recruiters for his quarterbacking abilities.

"By the time I was a senior I was 6-foot-4, 200 pounds," he recalled. "And back in those days, there weren't many 6-foot-4, 200-pound quarterbacks around."

The late Don Hertler had the privilege of coaching Snyder in football and baseball.

"Dick was an excellent baseball player," Hertler said in 1989. "He was great in the field. He had a good fastball but also had control. As a hitter, he could hit the low pitches better than most people. Dick was also an excellent passer. We didn't throw much back then, though. It just wasn't customary for any team. We had Dick roll out a lot and gave him the option of throwing the ball or running it himself."

"Because football was so big in Stark County everyone assumed I was going to play football in college," Snyder said.

Snyder received football scholarship offers from schools such as Ohio State University and the University of Michigan.

"But when it came down to putting the final signatures on the papers those schools who wanted me for football didn't want me to play baseball in the spring," he said.

Ironically, one of Snyder's finest performances on the football field was the springboard to his future on the basketball court.

"I think we were playing at West Branch my senior year," he recalled. "I scored four or five touchdowns—a couple of them I might've thrown for. A guy named Don Davidson—I think that was his name—was at the game. His son had played basketball for West Branch and was playing for a little school in North Carolina at the time called Davidson College. The coach there was Lefty Driesell [the future University of Maryland basketball coach]. I didn't even know the guy, but when Don saw me at the football game he must've known who I was from my playing basketball because he called Lefty down at Davidson and told him about me."

Driesell came to watch Snyder play and liked what he saw. He wanted him bad. Snyder averaged 20.7 points per game his senior year. He graduated in 1962. He gave up football and accepted a full scholarship to play basketball for Davidson. He played baseball there, too, but soon realized that a professional basketball career was really in his future.

After averaging more than 20 points per game on the Wildcats' freshman team, Snyder became a starter at small forward on the varsity squad his sophomore year and averaged 12 points per contest, helping his team to a 22–4 record. His scoring average rose to 18 per game the next year as Davidson finished 24–2 and shot up to nearly 30 per game his senior year, a season in which Snyder, an All-American that year, and his teammates finished 21–7, won the school's first Southern Conference Championship, and advanced to its first-ever NCAA Tournament. The 'Cats lost 94–78 to Syracuse in the East Regional Semifinals after defeating Rhode Island 95–65 in the first round.

Snyder's steady offensive improvement was complemented by his tenacious defense.

"I always got the toughest defensive assignments," he said. "I received a lot of notoriety for my defense. Lefty taught us good defensive fundamentals. We played man-to-man 100 percent of the time."

Snyder graduated in 1966 with a degree in business. That summer he was chosen by the St. Louis (now Atlanta) Hawks in the second round of the NBA Draft, the 14th player overall. He spent two seasons as a shooting guard for a Hawks team that qualified for the postseason both years, advancing to the Western Division Finals in his rookie season of 1966–67. He was traded to expansion Phoenix and averaged more than 12 points per game in 1968–69 for the sorry Suns at small forward, but was traded to the Seattle SuperSonics early the next season. Back at shooting guard, where he would remain for the rest of his career, Snyder enjoyed some individual success in the Pacific Northwest, never averaging fewer than 13 points per game. In 1970–71 he netted a career-best 19.4 points per contest. Unfortunately, the Sonics had just one winning season and failed to qualify for the playoffs while he was there. Snyder played under future Cavaliers guard and head coach Lenny Wilkens in his first three years in Seattle and under legendary Celtics great Bill Russell in his last season there, before being traded to the Cavs soon after the 1973–74 season ended. Snyder was surprised at the move, to say the least.

"I'd played for five years in Seattle," he said. "At that point, my family and I had started to get comfortable enough and I was liked well enough that we thought, 'I might end my career in Seattle.' And Bill expressed satisfaction and was pleased with what I'd done, especially in the second half of my last season there."

Snyder averaged 18.1 points, 3.6 assists, and a career-high 4.1 rebounds per game during that '73–74 campaign.

"I was going to a team that I didn't feel had a very good chance to win," he said. "I'd also heard a lot of negative things about Bill Fitch."

Snyder grudgingly came to Cleveland.

"What options did I have? At that point I didn't have a whole lot of leverage," he said. "I mean, I was a solid player but I wasn't an All-Star, a player who was well known around the country. So my feeling was that, if I wanted to continue my career, I didn't have a whole lot that I could do to force a trade someplace else. I'm not a belligerent type of guy anyway. I understood that it was a business. It turned out that many of those things I'd heard about Fitch were true. I didn't agree with a lot of his coaching philosophy and some of his actions off the court. He would criticize his own players publicly, to the press, all the time."

The Cavaliers traded for the 6-foot-5, 207-pound Snyder because former Notre Dame All-American Austin Carr had become ravaged by injuries. Then, two months into Snyder's first season in Cleveland, A.C. suffered his worst injury yet—a career-changing one to his right knee.

"Austin was at a point in his career where, if we gave him too many minutes, he might've gone back to being a cripple again," Fitch recalled. "We couldn't use him for 40 minutes [per game] anymore. We also got Dick because we needed the outside game. I've always said that Dick Snyder came into the league about 10 years too soon. If he'd have come in 10 [actually 13] years later, he would've probably been in the record books somewhere along the line as a three-point shooter. He could've really developed that part of his game had we had the three-point shot back when he was playing. If you set a pick and got Dick free, he was gonna knock it."

"You just couldn't leave him alone," Mike Peticca said. "He was as reliable at knocking down the open middle range jumper as most anybody in the league."

"Dick also knew how to get to the foul line," Nate Thurmond added.

Snyder was a force defensively, too.

"I think his all-around game wasn't as recognized as it should've been," said Peticca. "He was a big, strong defender. He got right in people's faces."

"What I liked about Dick was, if we needed him to, he could guard the small forwards," said Fitch. "He was smart, so you could put him in a team defense, and if we were doing a lot of switching or making rotations, which we did a lot, he was a big help."

A starter for most of his time with the Cavs, Snyder found the atmosphere around the team was much better than what he had been experiencing in Seattle.

"There'd been quite a lot of turmoil in my next-to-last year there after they basically fired [player-coach] Lenny or forced him out," he said. "We had three coaches in a two-year span and an influx of players who . . . weren't exactly, uh . . . well, we had some locker-room situations that you'd rather not be a part of. I found that the guys I was playing with in Cleveland were great."

Despite being a family man with a wife and children by that time, and not someone who went clubbing with his single teammates after games, Snyder fit in well with his new team.

"Dick didn't have an easy job coming in there," said Fitch. "He was an older player who'd been to a lot of places now playing with a bunch of young guys, but he made the adjustment as well as could be expected. I have a lot of respect for Dick."

"I think I had a certain level of respect from some of the players," Snyder said. "At that point, pretty much everybody knew what I could and couldn't do. I could shoot the jump shot, I could run the court, I could work hard defensively. They knew I wasn't going to dazzle anybody with my playmaking skills, though."

Snyder was as focused as could be, as he was throughout his entire career.

"My attitude was, I was fighting for survival every night," he said. "You're pass or fail on your own merits on the floor."

"Dick understood the game extremely well so he could fit in in any situation. He was a consummate pro," Thurmond said.

Snyder arrived in Cleveland at just the right time when it came to the team itself.

"We were moving into The Coliseum, so it was a new venue," he said. "Also, my folks and my wife's family could come see the games because they were all still living in North Canton."

What's more, winning was right around the corner for the young Cavaliers, a team that had not won more than 32 games in any of its first four seasons. Snyder averaged 14.2 points per game in his first season in Cleveland, helping the Cavs to a 40–42 record that nearly landed them in the playoffs. Then came the unforgettable Miracle of Richfield season in which he hung up 12.6 points per contest. His scoring average continued to dwindle the next two seasons, which saw the team finish above .500 both years but fall in the first round of the playoffs each time. Snyder returned to Seattle as a free agent for one last hurrah before calling it quits.

"Lenny was back coaching there again and he had a young team with few veterans, so he felt he needed one more experienced player," he said. "That team was hungry. After making it to the championship the year before, they wanted to win it."

Snyder was a part of Seattle's first-ever major sports championship—albeit in a minor role—as the SuperSonics won the 1979 NBA title, defeating Washington, the team that had beaten them for the championship the year before.

Snyder was a member of the inaugural induction class of the Davidson College Athletics Hall of Fame in 1990. He was enshrined into the Ohio Basketball Hall of Fame in 2011. These days, he works as an agent for State Farm Insurance in Phoenix. He and his wife Terie have two grown sons.

"I'm glad I got a chance to coach Dick," Fitch said. "He was an important part of our ball club. He hit some big baskets for us."

None bigger than "The Shot" 40 years ago.

14 | Jim Chones

What if Jim Chones hadn't broken his foot? It is a question that will be asked forever.

The Cavaliers had just beaten Washington in a dramatic, seven-game Eastern Conference Semifinal playoff series. It took three miraculous wins for the Cavs to beat the Bullets. Not only was Chones Cleveland's leading scorer against Washington, he was its leading scorer during the 1975–76 regular season. He was a huge part of the Cavaliers' success that year.

Then the 6-foot-11, 245-pound Chones, the Cavaliers' starting center, broke his right foot while simply running down the court in a practice session just two days before the Cavs were to open the Conference Finals against the Celtics in Boston. He was done for the season. Nate Thurmond took his place and played as well as he could in the starting role against the Celtics. It was just a little too much, however, for his 34-year-old body to handle. The Cavs lost in six tough games, then watched Boston beat a gallant, but still just a 42-win, Phoenix team in the Finals. Just about anyone who is asked, whether a teammate of Chones, Bill Fitch, media members, or fans, offers the same answer to the question asked above: "The Cavs would've won the NBA Championship had Chones not broken his foot." Chones himself feels the same way.

"We'd have won the whole thing," he said.

Chones's long road to the shores of Lake Erie began on November 30, 1949, in Racine, Wisconsin, a city of some 70,000 people at the time that lies right on Lake Michigan.

"There was a lot of manual labor there, a lot of foundries and factories," Chones said. "At one time, we were the most industrialized city per capita in the United States."

Chones gained an interest in athletics at an early age.

"My first love was football," he said, "but I was a string bean then and kept getting hurt. I was trying to tackle guys but I'd hurt myself more than them, so I switched to basketball. I'd go to the playgrounds and watch the older kids play and I liked the movement, the up and down the court. I started playing when I was around 11 years old at the YMCA on Saturday mornings. I didn't know how to shoot yet, but I was always taller than the other kids so I could rebound the ball.

"I used to watch the Celtics play on our black-and-white TV with my dad. I'd get between his legs and we'd sit there and watch. One day when I was 12 or 13 he looked down at me and said, 'Jim, you can do that.' I got ready to disagree but before I could get 'no' out, he slapped me upside the head and said, 'You're a Chones, you can do anything.' And I looked up at him and said, 'Okay.' I'd already been playing a little bit, but that really spanked it into my brain that 'Maybe I *can* do this.'"

Chones had a couple of close friends—older buddies—who, in a sense, became his own personal coaches.

"A guy named Wally Booker, who was a cross country guy but who also played high school basketball, took an interest in me at about that time," he said. "And another guy named Danny Peterson who went to a high school called St. Catherine's took an interest in me, too. After school I'd go up to the playground and they'd teach me how to play: 'Oh no, you've got to put your elbow in, you've got to play defense. C'mon, you can block that shot!' And I'd say, 'What do you mean block that shot?' So they showed me how to block shots, and I started playing more."

As a freshman, the 6-foot-2 Chones attended Franklin Junior High School where he was the best player on the team. By the time he entered his sophomore year at Park High School, he had grown to 6-foot-6.

"My junior year we lost in the regionals to a team I know we should've beaten, and I took it personally," he said. "I wasn't satisfied, so I went to my father one day and said, 'Dad, I've been playing basketball with a guy named Wally Booker.' And my dad said, 'Yeah, I know him from down south. His father works on the line with me at the foundry.' I said, 'Wally and this guy named Danny Peterson, who I've also been playing with, told me if I want to go to a big university I should go to St. Catherine's my senior year.' Even though it was much smaller than Park, which was a public school, St. Catherine's High School had been perennial title contenders in the Catholic schools state tournament. It had even won the national Catholic tournaments in Boston and New York quite a few times. A few players from St. Catherine's had gone on to play at Loyola Chicago, a school with a great basketball tradition at the time."

There was a problem, though, namely Chones's coach at Park, Don Gardner.

"Coach Gardner told me that I was only good enough to play at the small colleges," Chones said, "local schools like La Crosse and Stevens Point. But I knew I could play against better players than that. Coach Gardner didn't know that in the summers Wally and Danny would take me up to Milwaukee where I played against future NBA star 'Downtown' Freddy Brown; John Johnson, who would be the Cavs' first-ever draft pick; and a lot of other college guys. And he didn't know that I had another friend who'd take me down to Chicago around the time when I was a junior to play against some of the Chicago Bulls like Bob Love. So I knew I could play Division I college ball and I told that to Coach Gardner. He said, 'No, you're a small-school player.' My junior year, in addition to several offers from small schools, I had about 10 offers from big-time schools. But Coach said, 'Don't consider those. Just fill out the ones for the small schools.' I didn't do it, though, because I knew I was better."

Chones transferred to St. Catherine's in the spring of his junior year. It was the best decision he ever made.

"I had an easy time fitting in there because it was right in the inner city," he said. "There weren't many black kids there, though, maybe 15–20—and I think I was the only one on the basketball team. I could walk home. It was only about six blocks so it was in my neighborhood. I felt comfortable. The coach, John McGuire, also made it comfortable. At the time, McGuire was one of the three winningest high school coaches in all of Wisconsin. He was very influential to me. I knew who he was and he knew who I was, but we didn't meet in person until I got there. I had to finish the school year out. I was behind in a few subjects so Coach Gardner said, 'Look, in order for you to play Division I ball you need to do this, this, and that.' They connected me with one of the nuns at a place called Dominicans— The Sisters of Siena at an NAIA school called Dominican College that was only three miles away. They'd tutor me in math and English so I could get my grades up. And I did."

The move to St. Catherine's changed everything for Chones. Just the simple fact that he would be playing his senior year there turned into a bonanza for him. Word spread across the country.

"When I got to school on the first day of my senior year," he said, "I had about 300 [scholarship] offers waiting for me. Coach McGuire said to me, 'This is your mail from over the summer.' I had four boxes—four boxes!— full of letters, including one from UCLA, but none from any of the black schools because, I was told later, and it's kind of amusing, they all thought I was white because of my name—C-H-O-N-E-S—and because I was at a Catholic school."

That year, Chones averaged in the vicinity of 25 points and 15 rebounds per game, leading St. Catherine's to an undefeated season and the Wisconsin Catholic schools state title.

"In the tournament," he said, "I played against three very big guys."

Chones was the Player of the Year in Wisconsin (including public schools) and was an All-American. As for where he would hone his skills in college, it came down to Michigan State University and Marquette University.

"I'd declared that I was going to Michigan State," he said. "I'd given an oral commitment but the coach there, John Benington, died while playing racquetball that summer. So I asked to be let out of it because I loved the guy, and they let me out. About a week later Marquette called. Al McGuire came down with Senator [Herb] Kohl, his best friend whose family founded what is now Kohl's department stores. The only sales pitch McGuire gave my dad was, 'If Jimmy does what I tell him to do he'll be a pro.'"

Chones accepted a full scholarship to play for Marquette.

"If I'd stayed at Park for my senior year," he said, "I probably would've never gone to Marquette."

Chones started at center in 1969–70 on the Warriors' freshman team, which lost just one game. By his sophomore year he had grown to 6-foot-10. That season, he averaged 17.9 points and a team-leading 11.5 rebounds per game, helping Marquette to a 28–1 record. The team, which had won the NIT the year before, won its 39th straight game when it beat Miami (Ohio) 62–47 in the first round of the NCAA Tournament. Then came a 60–59 heartbreaking defeat to underdog Ohio State in a Mideast Regional Semifinal.

"Dean Meminger, our All-American guard and leading scorer fouled out of that game," Chones said. "He'd never fouled out of a game in his life. And they fouled him out. I had a hatred for officials from then on."

The next year, Chones made First-Team All-American when he hung up both a team-leading 20.6 points and 11.9 rebounds per game as Marquette went 25–4. The Warriors beat Ohio 73–49 in an NCAA tourney first-round game before bowing out with an 85–69 loss to Kentucky in a Mideast Regional Semifinal.

Asked what it was like to play for the legendary Al McGuire, Chones chuckled.

"It was interesting," he said. "Al wore his attitude on his shoulders. It was his program, he did it his way. He didn't want anybody who was soft.

He believed in 'I hit you first, don't you wait to be hit back,' so we were always aggressive. That had been the mentality with all of his teams. If you ever saw an Al McGuire team play, it might've been a little undersized but it was always the aggressor. We attacked on defense, we attacked on offense. Al McGuire was a tough coach. You respected him because he never said anything that was B.S. He always told you the way it was."

In March of Chones's junior year, his father died of cancer at just 43 years of age. That prompted Chones to leave Marquette immediately, becoming only the second player in NCAA history to flee school early for the pros, before his graduating year.

"I had five brothers and sisters who I had to take care of," he said. "My mother worked at a great Italian restaurant and brought leftovers home but that wasn't enough, so I left. I was made an offer by the ABA. Someone called me and told me to go down to this attorney's office, so I went down there and there was an offer sheet for millions of dollars to play for the New York Nets under [former, and future, St. John's University head coach] Lou Carnesecca."

Chones signed the deal. As a power forward in 1972–73, he averaged 11.4 points and 7.1 rebounds per game for a Nets team that finished 30–54 but still qualified for the playoffs, losing to the Carolina Cougars four games to one in the first round. Chones was voted to the ABA All-Rookie First Team. That spring, he was chosen by the Los Angeles Lakers in the second round of the NBA Draft, but he instead opted to play in 1973–74 for Carolina, to whom he had been traded by New York, under head coach Larry Brown, who would go on to a long and distinguished head-coaching career in the pros and in the college ranks.

"The Nets had to make room for some bum named Julius Erving," laughed Chones, who averaged 14.8 points and 7.8 rebounds per game in helping the Cougars to a 47–37 finish that unfortunately resulted in a four-game sweep by the Kentucky Colonels in the Eastern Division Semifinals. "L.A. held my rights for a year, and after that, I'd become a free agent. I wanted out of Carolina because I wanted to get as far away as I could from Larry Brown. He was a great coach but he could be annoying, especially to young players. The ABA was falling apart anyway and two years later would dissolve four teams into the NBA. I wanted to get in the NBA and prove myself. Carolina gave me a release, before I became a free agent, and Cleveland bought my rights from the Lakers. That was the first negotiated deal between the NBA and ABA."

Chones had known Fitch for years upon his arrival in Cleveland.

"When Bill was at Minnesota," Chones said, "he recruited me at the same time Marquette was recruiting me. Marquette had an end-of-the-

Jim Chones goes for the bucket over Atlanta's Bill Willoughby, January 15, 1976. (The Cleveland Press Collection, Michael Schwartz Library, Cleveland State University)

season banquet so they invited all of the prospects and recruits, so I went up, and who was the guest speaker? Bill Fitch. At the end of the talk he said, 'Jim Chones, if you don't go to Minnesota go to Marquette,' and everybody started laughing."

Chones made an immediate impact with the Cavaliers, hanging up 14.5 points and a team-leading 9.4 rebounds per game in a 1974–75 season that saw the team improve by 11 games from the year before and miss its first playoff berth ever by a single game. Then came the Miracle of Richfield season in which Chones, or "Sweets," as he was known due to his sweet jump shot, led the team with 15.8 points per game and hauled down nine rebounds per contest. Soon after came his infamous foot injury during that year's playoffs. He was healthy again and back to full form when the 1976–77 season arrived. He led the Cavs in 1977–78 and '78–79 with 10.3 rebounds per game each season.

"Chones was a very, very good center," Thurmond said. "He had extreme confidence in his ability. He had an attitude that nobody could stop him as far as him scoring, and he had a nice repertoire of shots."

"I thought Jim really developed over his time with the Cavaliers," Dick Snyder said. "I thought he was very talented."

Chones was traded to the Lakers just prior to the start of the 1979–80 season to back up Kareem Abdul-Jabbar at center and Spencer Haywood at power forward. He wound up, though, starting at power forward and was a key contributor that season and the next due to Haywood's health issues.

"We rolled my first year there," he said. "Magic [Johnson] was a rookie. We had a very talented team. We won the title and I got my ring."

Traded to Washington after the 1980–81 season in which the Lakers were ousted by underdog Houston in the first round of the playoffs, Chones backed up youngsters Jeff Ruland and Rick Mahorn in D.C. in 1981–82, then played in Italy for a year before retiring. He spent 10 seasons as the color analyst for local televised Cavaliers games before entering the stockbroking profession. In the meantime, he kept his broadcasting bubbles burning as the color analyst for SEC games on ESPN. In 2007 he returned to the Cavs as a radio postgame analyst. When usual Cavaliers radio voice Joe Tait missed much of the 2010–11 season due to health problems, Chones and Mike Snyder replaced him as the interim announcing team. Chones became a full-time member of the radio crew the next year, working with new play-by-play man John Michael. Chones said he owes a ton of credit to Tait for the success he has enjoyed in the broadcast business, mainly on the radio end.

"Joe was my first teacher," he said. "He took me under his wing and showed me how to broadcast radio."

A 2002 inductee into the Greater Cleveland Sports Hall of Fame, Chones returned to Marquette that same year to earn his degree in philosophy. He and his wife Elores have been married for 41 years. They live in Cleveland.

"Elores is the MVP of our family," he said. "If it wasn't for her, I don't know where I'd be right now."

The Choneses have five grown children, triplet sons and two daughters. In fact, both daughters are employed in the NBA—the oldest, Kareeda, in the front office of the Milwaukee Bucks and the other, Kaayla, in the Minnesota Timberwolves' front office. All three sons attended Ivy League, or Baby Ivy League, schools—one went to Brown University; the other two went to Colgate University.

"All five of my kids played college basketball," Proud Papa said. "We're the only family in NCAA history to have six family members play Division I sports."

During his days as a Cavalier, Chones was known for his smooth moves not only on the basketball court but also on the dance floor.

"I'm one of the best of all time," he said.

As for hobbies, Chones enjoys playing his bass guitar and writing short stories. He is in the process of authoring three novels, too. Perhaps one should "center" around a 6-foot-11, 245-pound Cavaliers player who does *not* break his foot just prior to the Conference Finals against the Celtics.

At least then there would be a happy ending.

15 | Bingo Smith

There likely would never have been a Miracle of Richfield had it not been for Bingo Smith's "Stunner in Landover."

The Cavaliers had lost Game 1 of their 1976 Eastern Conference Semi-final series to the Washington Bullets—at home, no less. Two nights later on April 15 at the Capital Centre in Landover, Maryland, the Cavs were well aware that they needed to win Game 2 or they would trail the Bullets two games to none. With his team down 79–78, Smith took a mid-court inbounds pass from Jim Cleamons and nailed a 25-footer with two seconds to go, which gave the Cavs an eventual, and remarkable, 80–79 victory. Smith's heroics lifted the Cavs' spirits en route to a 4–3 series triumph.

Smith, whose given name is Robert, was born on February 26, 1946, in Memphis, Tennessee. He attended Melrose High School where he was a star not only in basketball but also in baseball, football, and track and field. The youngest of seven children, Smith was the first four-sport letter-man in the state of Tennessee. He was All-State as a forward in basketball, as a pitcher and first baseman in baseball, and as a flanker and safety in football. He was the city high jump and long jump champ four years in a row.

"I had 424 scholarship offers for all four sports," Smith said. "I could've gone to Arizona, Kansas, UCLA, Nebraska . . . I could've been the first black to go to Alabama. I could've signed with the Pittsburgh Pirates my junior year, but my mother wouldn't let me. She wanted me to go to college."

Smith wound up accepting a full ride to play basketball at the University of Tulsa.

"My mother was getting tired of me not being able to make up my mind. She was going crazy," he said. "Schools had been calling at all times of the night and day and she just couldn't take it anymore. So one day I told her, 'I'll tell you what. The very next call that comes in, that's where I'm going to school.' And, sure enough, the assistant head basketball coach from Tulsa, Ken Hayes, called and offered me a full scholarship, the last one he had left. He was going to sign this boy from Florida. I said, 'You come see me now and talk to my mother, I'll sign with you today.' So he came over that afternoon while on his way to Florida. I think what sold my mother on Tulsa was that Coach Hayes didn't say anything about any cars or houses . . . the only thing he talked about was that I'd get a good education. He told me to sign the paper and I said, 'Okay,' and I signed it. I knew nothing about Tulsa, I just wanted to satisfy my mother. And that was that."

Smith averaged 15 points per game while starting at small forward on the Golden Hurricane's freshman team, which finished 15–0 and beat by 20-some points the school that had won the National Junior College championship the year before. Starting at small forward on the varsity team as a sophomore in 1966–67, Smith averaged 15 points and a team-leading 10.4 rebounds per game, helping Tulsa to a 19–8 record and a second-place finish in the Missouri Valley Conference. The next season, Smith played on a broken foot—"just a hairline fracture," he said—for most of the season but still went for 13.1 points and 7.3 rebounds per game as the Golden Hurricane slipped to an 11–12 record. He was invited to the 1968 Summer Olympic trials but had to decline because he was still recovering from his foot injury. He remembered Hayes, who had replaced Joe Swank as head coach after his junior year, calling him into his office one day prior to the start of his senior season.

"Coach said, 'Bobby, I'm gonna let you play your brand of basketball,'" he said. "And that really got me excited. I'd been playing in the wrong system under the previous coach. He'd wanted no superstars or nothin'. Coach Hayes promised me that he'd let me play like I had in high school, a more wide-open offensive attack, when I averaged 32 points per game my senior year. He let me shoot the ball more."

Smith took full advantage of his coach's game plan. He averaged a team-best 24.5 points per game and hauled down 10.3 boards per contest as Tulsa improved to 19–8 and third place in the MVC. He was First-Team All-Conference and graduated in 1969 with a degree in psychology/education. Smith was shocked when he was taken by the San Diego Rockets with the sixth overall pick in the '69 NBA Draft.

"I'd have been happy if I was drafted in the third round," he said.

Smith was also chosen by the Kentucky Colonels in the first round of the ABA Draft. It did not take him long to make a decision—he was off to sunny Southern California.

"Kentucky offered me more money," he said, "but it was the NBA!"

Asked if he had a "Welcome to the NBA moment" during his rookie season of 1969–70, Smith did not hesitate before answering.

"We were playing Seattle in an exhibition game," he said. "I was guarding Tom Meschery, a guy who'd been in the league for almost 10 years. We were running down the court, and Meschery just popped me in the mouth with his elbow on purpose and bloodied my nose. I ran back to the bench and told my coach, Jack McMahon, 'My nose is bleeding.' He looked at me and said, 'We don't stop play because you're bleeding!' So I ran back down the court, and while I was going for a rebound I punched Meschery on the back of his head. As soon as I hit him someone told me that this guy, Meschery, is the only guy who'd ever been in a fight with Wilt Chamberlain. So I'm saying, 'Wow! What have I done?' Meschery looked at me and said, 'You'll be alright, you'll make it.'"

Smith backed up veteran small forward Don Kojis for about the first two-thirds of his rookie year before replacing Kojis, who broke his foot, for the rest of the season. That season ended with San Diego in last place in the Western Division with a league-worst 27–55 record. Smith was not exactly thrilled when he learned that the Rockets made him available for the 1970 Expansion Draft in which the Cavaliers, along with Buffalo and Portland, would have their shots at him.

"San Diego," he said, "figured that since I didn't play much my rookie year, I wouldn't be taken in the Expansion Draft, that the three new teams would take players who were more established."

The Rockets were wrong. The 6-foot-5, 195-pound Smith was chosen by the Cavs. He wasn't happy about it, either.

"I wanted to stay in San Diego," he said. "I was going to have a chance to start the next year! When I was told I was going to Cleveland I said, 'Cleveland?' I don't think I knew where Cleveland was! I just knew there was a lot of cold weather and snow there and that Jim Brown had played there, but he was retired so I wouldn't get a chance to see him."

"Bingo," as Smith was known to Cavaliers fans mainly by way of Joe Tait and whose nickname had originated in college due to his radar outside shot, was the team's starting small forward from the start. Whether he was playing for a Cavs team that won just 15 games in their first season of 1970–71, for the Miracle of Richfield team, or for his last full-season Cavs team in 1978–79 that won just 30 games, Smith was always the same, as steady as could be.

Bingo Smith closely guards Golden State's Rick Barry in the season opener, October 23, 1975. (The Cleveland Press Collection, Michael Schwartz Library, Cleveland State University)

He averaged 13.2 points and 4.2 rebounds per game in his nine-plus seasons with the club and was its leading scorer in 1974–75 at 15.9 points per contest.

"Bingo had a sweet shot, the best jump shot on the team no question," Nate Thurmond said. "We had a lot of confidence in him. He could shoot it from the locker room."

Added Dick Snyder, another good shooter, "Bingo would take the shots that not many guys were shooting then that everybody shoots now, the runners off of one foot, almost what they call floaters today, instead of pulling up and shooting a form jump shot."

"When you look at Bingo's shooting percentages [45.2 overall with the Cavs]," said Mike Peticca, "they're pretty impressive because he didn't get many points running the break or driving to the basket. He just added a dimension that was very valuable that every team has to have."

"Defensively," Thurmond said, "Bingo could get after people, too. He had a lot of pride in that."

"Rick Barry of the Warriors was maybe the best shooter in the league," said Sheldon Ocker, "and he was probably the most temperamental player in the league. Nobody liked him. He didn't like to be touched, and Bingo was the guy who guarded him when the Cavs played the Warriors. And Bingo would put his hands on Barry just to annoy him. Barry would be brushing Bingo's hands away. It would really affect Barry's game when he had to go up against Bingo."

Eight games into the 1979–80 season Smith was traded back to San Diego, but not to the Rockets, who had since relocated to Houston. He was now a member of the Clippers, the former Buffalo Braves who had moved out West during the 1978 offseason. Smith was taken by the Dallas Mavericks in the 1980 Expansion Draft and lasted until the final cut. He then retired.

A 1984 inductee into the Tulsa Athletics Hall of Fame and whose number 7 is retired by the Cavaliers, Smith worked as a bank manager, as the recreation director at a boys detention center, and as the director at a recreation center, all in the Cleveland area. He became ill in 1996 and has survived a heart attack and three strokes. Smith has four daughters and a son and five grandchildren. He lives in Akron.

"Bingo Smith," Bill Fitch said, "was light years ahead of where he should've been because he had that three-point range. He was deadly."

16 | Jim Brewer

Every NBA team needs an enforcer, someone to police the area when "extracurricular activities," or foul play, arise. Jim Brewer was just that man while playing for the Cavaliers from 1973–79. "Jim was a hard-nosed guy," said Les Levine.

However, the 6-foot-9, 210-pound Brewer, a power forward for Cleveland who was selected with the second overall pick in the 1973 NBA Draft, was more than just a cop on the court. He was also a darned good player.

"Jim was a prototype power forward," Dick Snyder said. "He was exactly what those 1970s Cavs teams needed because he'd go out and play defense against the other team's power forward or scoring forward if they had any size at all. Jim was also a great offensive rebounder. He always seemed to be around the basket. Of the guys I played with, he was probably second during my career only to Paul Silas as an offensive rebounder."

"He could bang around," said Nate Thurmond. "He took care of the boards for us when I wasn't in there. He was also good defensively, he knew how to position himself. He didn't block shots but still could stop people from scoring."

"Jim's defense was awesome," Joe Tait said.

"Jim also knew what shots he should take and what shots he shouldn't take," Thurmond said. "He shot the ball from about 10–12 feet. He would knock that face-up jumper down pretty regularly. He knew he wasn't out there to shoot but if the opportunity arose, he'd take the shot."

Born on December 3, 1951, in the Chicago suburb of Maywood, Brewer, the second youngest of seven children, gained an interest in baseball, not basketball, at a very young age. He attended "baseball school," a day camp, for two summers when he was 7 and 8 years old. After that, he entered Little League in which he mainly played center field. Soon, Brewer started shooting hoops and developed a fondness for basketball. He went out for the Washington Elementary School team when he was in the sixth grade and made the squad. He worked hard at it and enjoyed the exercise but was not very good.

Brewer's love for basketball really blossomed during the summer between eighth and ninth grade. He would practice all day, every day. His coordination was improving, he was scoring more, and he was becoming more physical. A growth spurt didn't hurt. Besides playing forward and center on the freshman "A" team at Proviso East High School, that year Brewer also played football and baseball. The varsity basketball coach pulled him aside, however, and told him that injuries from football could keep his basketball career from prospering. He listened to his coach and gave up football, and baseball, too. Everything started to come together. He was elevated from the Pirates' junior varsity team to varsity as a forward halfway through his sophomore year.

In his last two years Brewer was the starting center. As a senior in 1968–69, he averaged around 16 points per game and led Proviso East to its first-ever state championship at a time when the state tournament was still all-inclusive, meaning every single high school in Illinois—no matter the size—was in the tourney. Even more impressive was that Brewer played in the semifinal and championship games with a twisted ankle. In 2007, the Illinois High School Association named Brewer one of the 100 legends of the IHSA Boys Basketball Tournament.

A career in the NBA was the farthest thing from Brewer's mind. He was focused on where he would play in college. Schools across the country recruited him, including the University of Illinois, UCLA, the University of North Carolina, and the University of Minnesota. It came down to Illinois and Minnesota. In fact, Brewer was recruited by Minnesota via Golden Gophers head coach Bill Fitch, who a year later left to take the Cavaliers' head-coaching job but would reunite with Brewer in Cleveland three years after that. Brewer was swayed by Minnesota's urban Minneapolis setting over rural Champaign. Also, Minnesota was close enough so his parents could watch him play but far enough away so he could relax and not be held to such a high standard.

Thus it was on to the Twin Cities, where Brewer, who was 6-foot-7 by then, played on Minnesota's freshman team before starting at forward as a sophomore and at center as a junior and senior for the Golden Gophers. He was a teammate of future Major League Baseball Hall of Famer Dave Winfield his last two years. Brewer averaged 16.6 points and a team-leading 13.8 rebounds per game as a sophomore. As a junior, he netted 9.8 points

Jim Brewer against the Warriors with Austin Carr below, 1976. (Courtesy of AndersonsClevelandDesign.com)

and a team-high 11 rebounds per contest, helping his team to an 18–7 overall record and an 11–3 mark in the Big Ten, which gave it the conference title and a berth in the NCAA Tournament. The Gophers lost 70–56 to Florida State in a Mideast Regional Semifinal. Earlier that season, on January 25, Brewer was involved in a vicious brawl between the Gophers and visiting Ohio State, and future Cavs teammate Luke Witte, that ended in a Buckeyes forfeit victory and hospital stays for Witte and two of his teammates. Brewer averaged 14.1 points and a team-leading 11.6 rebounds per game his senior year as Minnesota finished 21–5 overall and 10–4 and in second place in the Big Ten. Brewer's number 52 is retired by the University of Minnesota.

Brewer was also a member of the United States' 1972 Summer Olympic team, which lost by one point to the Soviet Union in the infamous—and controversial—gold medal game in Munich, West Germany. "Brew," as he was known, enjoyed his finest NBA season in the Miracle of Richfield year when he averaged career highs of 11.5 points and a team-leading 10.9 rebounds per game. The next season he also led the Cavs with 9.4 boards per contest.

The uncle of former NBA player and current Los Angeles Clippers president of basketball operations and head coach Doc Rivers, Brewer was traded to the Detroit Pistons in February 1979, also as a power forward, a position at which he would remain for the rest of his career. He was traded to the Portland Trail Blazers some three weeks before the start of the 1979–80 season and was dealt again to the Los Angeles Lakers two days prior to the start of the 1980–81 campaign. He was a backup in both Portland and L.A. but was a member of the Lakers' '81–82 title team. Brewer played in Italy through 1985 before calling it quits. He was an executive with the Minnesota Timberwolves from 1990–92.

"You'd think, because of his aggressiveness, that Jim's personality would've been that way, too, but it wasn't," Sheldon Ocker said. "He was just a real nice guy."

"Jim was a tough, tough guy who gave everything he had," said Tait, "but he was also a quiet player."

For someone his size, Brewer ran the floor exceptionally well.

"Jim could fill the lane and be one of the wing guys going to the basket on the fast break," said Snyder.

"Jim had a knack for making big plays—defensively *and* offensively—late in close games," Mike Peticca said. "If he would've had a little better of an offensive repertoire as far as being able to score, he'd be remembered as an outstanding all-around player."

17 | Foots Walker

Foots Walker may have been the shortest player on the Cavaliers during five of his six seasons with the team, but the 6-foot, 172-pound point guard certainly was not short on energy. A third-round draft pick of the Cavs in 1974 out of the State University of West Georgia (now the University of West Georgia) after two years at Vincennes Junior College in Indiana, Walker was full of pep, and he infused it to his teammates every second he was on the floor whether he was starting or backing up Jim Cleamons or Walt Frazier.

"Foots was a dynamite replacement, a high-energy guy," Bill Fitch said.

"He was super quick. He was a great guy to play with," said Dick Snyder, Walker's backcourt mate on many occasions. "He'd push the ball up the floor and get it to you if you were open."

In fact, Walker, who was born on May 21, 1951, in Southampton, New York, and led Southampton High School to 61 straight wins from 1967–70, was tops on the Cavaliers in assists in his last three seasons with the team. Included was a career-high eight per game, which ranked fifth in the entire NBA in 1979–80, his final season with the team.

When he was in college, Walker, whose given name is Clarence, led Vincennes to the 1972 National Junior College Athletic Association Division I Championship and the State University of West Georgia to the 1974 NAIA title. On both occasions he was named tournament MVP. Walker was also a 2012 inductee into the NJCAA Basketball Hall of Fame.

While in the NBA, Walker surprised opponents at times with his offensive skills.

"Foots could take it to the basket and he could hit the tough jump shot," Snyder said. "Like everybody else on the team, there were nights when he'd pick up the scoring if it was needed."

The more experience Walker got, the more he played. He averaged a career-best 10.1 points per game in 1978–79, a season in which he also finished fourth in the league in steals. The next season, on December 2, he recorded his second triple-double with 15 points, 11 assists, and 10 rebounds in a home win over Atlanta (his first triple-double was in his rookie season, also against the Hawks). Walker was traded to New Jersey some two weeks prior to the start of the 1980–81 season. He spent four years as a backup with the Nets before calling it quits.

"Foots just changed the tempo of the game so much," said Mike Peticca. "He was a terrific playmaker, and he had to be a nightmare to play against even though he wasn't a scorer first and foremost."

"Footsy was our engine, especially for that second squad," added Nate Thurmond. "He could dish it off and was good defensively because he had the long, long arms. He also had the biggest hands of any guy his size you'd ever see. And he was a hard worker."

According to Sheldon Ocker, Walker was the ultimate team player. "He added more to the team than just his individual skills," he said.

"I spoke to many of Foots's ex-teammates through the years for stories," said Bob Dolgan. "Everybody would say, 'How's Foots doin'?' and 'Tell Foots I said hello.' It was like he was the most popular guy on the team or almost the team leader."

"Foots is the only player I ever kissed on the floor," laughed Fitch. "We won a big game down in Atlanta when he made a heck of a play that saved the ball at the end of the game. He slid right under our bench at my feet as the game ended, and I hugged him and kissed him right on the cheek.

"And the guys never let me forget it."

18 | Austin Carr

Mr. Cavalier. That's who Austin Carr is known as to hundreds of thousands of Cavaliers fans. Ever since being chosen by the Cavs as the number-one overall selection in the 1971 NBA Draft and later venturing into the broadcast business as the team's television color commentator, A.C. has been all about the Cavaliers. He lives and dies with the Cavs.

However, long before he began putting points on the board and then making points on the air for the Cavs organization, Carr was quite possibly an even bigger star in the college ranks and, before that, at the high school level. He was born on March 10, 1948, in Washington, D.C. His father was a tremendous influence on him as he gained an interest in baseball, not basketball, when he was in the fifth grade.

"Besides being a good tennis player, my father was a good baseball player," Carr said. "He wanted to get into professional baseball, but that was about a year or two before Jackie Robinson got his opportunity to play in the big leagues. So he just never had the opportunity to play the game at that level. He'd tell us—me and my four brothers—about having to enter hotels through the back door and eating in places that you wouldn't want to eat."

Carr also began playing football in the fifth grade and, two years later, started playing basketball. He played competitively in all three sports through the Catholic Youth Organization and the Boys Club.

"We'd raise money for uniforms in the community," he said. "Baseball and football were my favorite sports. I played catcher in baseball and fullback and linebacker in football."

When Carr arrived at Mackin Catholic High School, he had to say farewell to football. "We only had about 250 students," he said, "so we couldn't have a team." Thus his focus turned to baseball and basketball, and soon after, basketball alone.

"Mackin was always a basketball powerhouse," said Carr, who was a starting guard on the varsity team all four years. "A lot of the guys would go to Division I schools. We played in the same league, the Washington, D.C., Catholic League, as DeMatha, a school that was, and still is, nationally known. We beat DeMatha for the league championship my senior year after having lost to them three years in a row, two of them in the title game. We traveled a lot my senior year and played some of the best high school teams in the country à la what LeBron James and Akron St. Vincent-St. Mary did his senior year."

Carr led Mackin in scoring in each of his last three years. As a senior, he was voted to the All-Met Team, which included the entire D.C. area—private *and* public schools—and was a Parade All-American. He was becoming quite an offensive threat who worked tirelessly at it.

"Anytime I had a chance to be in the gym or on the court, I was there," he said. "My brothers always used to tease me that I didn't have a girlfriend until I was a senior. I just didn't have time for it. I wanted to play ball and that was it. I was also lucky to get the type of coaching I got at the CYO, the Boys Club, and in high school. My high school coach was a pusher, and that kind of fit my personality because if we didn't shoot free throws well in a game and we lost to a team he felt we shouldn't have lost to, we'd come back in the gym after the game and practice. His attitude kind of fed right into what I was all about and I just worked, and shot the ball, to the point where I could do it in my sleep."

At the same time, Carr was dead set on earning his high school diploma. "My parents were sticklers for education," he said. "My mother went to two years of college and my father dropped out of school while in the 11th grade to support his family, so the one thing my parents always stressed was the fact that their kids were going to graduate from high school. I played the games, I loved the games that I played, but I had to make sure I got my diploma, too."

Schools across the country pursued Carr. It came down to the University of Notre Dame and the University of North Carolina.

"My family—both my mom and dad's sides—wanted me to go to North Carolina because they were all there," said Carr, "and my father wanted me to go to Notre Dame. My father won over the rest of my family."

Carr accepted a full scholarship to play for Notre Dame. He started at shooting guard on the Fighting Irish freshman team in 1967–68.

"We had a great year," he said. "We played the varsity eight times and beat them seven times, and they had a good year that season! The varsity coach just stopped the scrimmage one day because he got so frustrated, so fed up. We had seven or eight high school All-Americans on that freshman team. I averaged almost 35 points per game. If we lost a game, it was by accident."

As a sophomore, Carr averaged a team-leading 22 points and 5.3 rebounds per game in helping Notre Dame to a 20–7 record. The Fighting Irish fell, though, 63–60 to Miami (Ohio) in the first round of the NCAA Tournament.

The next two seasons Carr would put up such astronomical numbers scoring-wise, it was dizzying. As a junior in 1969–70 he averaged—yes, averaged!—a team-high 38.1 points and 8.1 rebounds per game, leading the Irish to a 21–8 record. In the first round of the NCAA tourney, Carr would give new meaning to a number that had earned a special place in the hearts of sports fans across the country. Nine years earlier, in 1961, Roger Maris had broken Babe Ruth's season home run record by belting 61 of them. In Notre Dame's first-round game against Ohio on March 7 in Dayton, Carr scored a jaw-dropping 61 points—still a tournament record—breaking Bill Bradley's mark by three, leading his team to a 112–82 victory. He had 35 points by halftime. He finished 25 of 44 from the field and 11 of 14 from the free-throw line. Even more remarkable is the fact that, had there been a three-point shot then, he would have dropped 73.

"For some reason," Carr said, "I just started out on a certain level in that game and I never stopped. That's just the way it went, it just kept going. The game kept going fast, and I just got into a flow and it just happened."

Carr wasn't done. In fact, he had just gotten started. Despite the Fighting Irish falling to Kentucky 102–99 in their next game, a Mideast Regional Semifinal, he hung up 52 points. Then in the regional third-place game he totaled 45 in a 121–106 loss to Iowa. He averaged 52.7 points—yes, 52.7 points!—per game in the 1970 tournament.

The next year Carr continued where he left off in 1969–70, netting a team-best 37.9 points and 7.3 rebounds per game, leading Notre Dame to a 20–9 record. One of those 20 wins was an 89–82 upset of UCLA, a program that was on its way to a fifth straight NCAA Championship and was in the midst of an incredible run of 10 titles in 12 years. Carr repeated his performance against Kentucky from the season before by scoring 52 points in a 102–94 triumph over Texas Christian in the first round of the NCAA Tournament. The Irish lost 79–72 to Drake in a Midwest Regional Semifinal and then were

Austin Carr while at Notre Dame. (Courtesy of AndersonsClevelandDesign.com)

beaten by Houston 119–106 in the regional's third-place game. Carr's prolific senior year did not go unnoticed. He was a First-Team All-American, the Associated Press College Basketball Player of the Year, and the Naismith College Player of the Year. Carr's career tournament-game scoring average was 41.3. He holds three of the top five scoring games in tourney history.

"You can make an argument," said Mike Peticca, "that Carr's one of the 10 or 20 best college players ever."

Carr's explanation for his success might be true, but it also shows how humble he is. "The era in which I came along is totally different than what college ball is now," he said. "College ball then was more like a proving ground for the pros. It's not like that now. When I came along, there was [Pete] Maravich, [Calvin] Murphy . . . guys who scored a lot. We may not have had a shot clock then, but we played up-tempo ball. This was well before slow-down ball unless it was the end of the game."

An economics major, Carr did not have any real thoughts of a career in the NBA until his senior year. "I just wasn't geared that way," he said. "I was geared more into getting my degree because of the way my parents pushed us. I knew I had a chance, but I didn't go to college just to play pro ball. I think my father was happier when I graduated from college than when I signed my first NBA contract."

Still, though, Carr knew he would be taken high in the 1971 NBA Draft. He just didn't know *how* high. "The word out," he said, "was that the Cavaliers were going to pick a big man—Elmore Smith, Sidney Wicks, or somebody like that. When I got out of my art history class on the first day of the Draft, I called my agent and he told me I was the first pick. It didn't really hit me about what it meant—that there's only one number-one pick each year and that can never be taken away from me—until I was further along in life. At first, I was just happy to be in the NBA, thankful."

As for his first training camp with the Cavs, the 6-foot-4, 200-pound Carr, who had also been drafted by the ABA's Virginia Squires that year, said that Bill Fitch pushed him and pushed him some more. "Bill didn't want me to feel that I had carte blanche for anything," he said, "so he always treated me like he treated everybody else. It didn't bother me because that's how my high school coach was. I was used to it, I was all for it. All I wanted to do was get better every day. I'd gone to Notre Dame, which was a football school, and I wanted to put basketball on the map there. I had the same feeling when I got to Cleveland. I knew it was a football town and that basketball was in its infancy there. I wanted to be part of making basketball a major sport there."

During the 1971 exhibition schedule Carr, the Cavs' starting shooting guard, broke his right foot and missed the first month of the season. Less than a month after returning to the court, he was sidelined again by another foot injury, missing another seven weeks. Upon his return, Carr began to display the skills that made him a star at Notre Dame and, despite missing almost half the season, was named to the 1971–72 NBA All-Rookie First Team. He averaged a team-leading 21.2 points per contest for a Cavs team that won just 23 games. After the season, he had surgery to clear up any recurring foot problems.

The arrival of veteran point guard Lenny Wilkens in 1972–73 gave Carr a solid partner in the backcourt and helped the Cavaliers improve by nine games. In fact, Carr and Wilkens both averaged a team-best 20.5 points per game.

"Playing with Lenny," Carr said, "was probably the most fortunate thing I had in my professional career because I learned so much from him about how to play guard and how to play the game."

Carr's finest season came the following year when he averaged a career-high 21.9 points per game while shooting 85.6 percent from the free-throw line, another career high, as he was voted to his only All-Star Game.

"Austin was an incredibly talented offensive player," said Dick Snyder. "He had the uncanny ability to either shoot the perimeter shot or take the ball to the hoop. He wasn't a great leaper, but he'd keep his dribble all the way to the basket and the big guys could never time his shot. So he could get to the hoop even though he wasn't super fast, and get the shot off, because he was strong enough to take a blow and still get the ball up in because nobody was sure when he was going to go up with the shot."

"Austin used his body as well as any guard other than Oscar Robertson at that time," Nate Thurmond said. "He could dribble, bang you off, and then step back and pop the shot. His wrists were so strong, his hands were big. And he could play some defense."

Some two months into the 1974–75 season Carr suffered a right knee injury that sidelined him for about half the season. "The knee basically blew up," he said.

Carr's absence likely prevented the Cavaliers from capturing their first-ever playoff berth, as they fell just one game short with a 40–42 record. Carr's weakened knee—he had four operations on it in all—resulted in him coming off the bench for the rest of his career.

"At first," he said, "it was tough because I drove myself to get back to starting, but I just wasn't the same player because of my knee. So I had to understand that, if I was going to play the game I loved any longer, it had to be off the bench because I just couldn't take it physically anymore. And I was fortunate enough to play in a system in which Coach Fitch would substitute four or five players at a time, and it worked. So that, along with what I'd learned from Lenny, even though he wasn't there anymore, really carried me through the rest of my career."

Carr managed to average double figures in scoring in each of the next five years—including 16.2 in 1976–77 and 17 in '78–79—the first three of which were playoff seasons, the penultimate one being the Miracle of Richfield campaign.

"Had he not gotten hurt," Joe Tait said, "Austin could've been a much, much more prolific ballplayer than he was, and he was pretty darned good as it was."

Selected by Dallas in the 1980 Expansion Draft, Carr spent 13 games with the Mavericks before getting sold to Washington, which waived him the following summer. Soon after, he retired.

"If Carr came along today and had that same injury," Les Levine said, "it'd be taken care of with some kind of arthroscopic surgery and he'd go on and be fine. He was a Hall of Famer without the injury. He was a shadow of himself after he got hurt. You could see him almost drag his leg sometimes. He was like a pitcher who lost his fastball and became a good curveball, crafty pitcher. That was Austin Carr. He changed his game completely when he had to."

"Not only would Carr have been a sure Hall of Famer without the injury," Peticca said, "he might've been a candidate to be one of the NBA's Top 50 players. Here's a guy who probably would've scored 20,000 points."

"Had Austin not gotten hurt," said Fitch, "there's no doubt we'd be talking about him in a lot bigger terms."

These days, Carr, whose number 34 is retired by the Cavaliers, serves as the team's director of community and business development and, of course, is its color analyst for broadcasts on Fox Sports Ohio. Some of his signature calls are:

- "He throws the hammer down!"
- "He hits it de-e-e-ep in The Q."
- "Get that weak stuff outta here!"

The following are more awards and honors bestowed upon Carr:

- 1980 Walter Kennedy Citizenship Award
- Greater Cleveland Sports Hall of Fame inductee (1992)
- National Collegiate Basketball Hall of Fame inductee (2007)

- 2011 Greater Cleveland Sports Commission Lifetime Achievement Award
- Notre Dame Basketball Ring of Honor (2011)
- 2014 Lower Great Lakes Emmy Award

Carr might not be an NBA Hall of Famer, but he is a Hall of Famer in Charlie Strasser's eyes.

"Austin was a class individual," Strasser said. "He was one of the hardest workers I've ever been around. He never said 'never,' never said 'no.' He always had a positive attitude."

"He was the shyest person I've ever seen," said Sheldon Ocker. "He was always really nice, but if you passed him in the hallway he'd turn his head the other way because he was too shy to speak! So anybody who would've told me he was going to be on TV, as he is now, I would've told them, 'You're crazy, there's no way Austin could be on TV.'"

Carr has undoubtedly overcome his shyness, to the point where his winning smile, engaging demeanor, insightful commentary, and obvious love for the Cavs shine through and are welcomed by fans into their living rooms night after night.

Mr. Cavalier would have it no other way. After all, Austin Carr bleeds wine, not red.

19 | Nate Thurmond

By the time Nate Thurmond joined the Cavaliers by way of a trade with the Chicago Bulls on Thanksgiving Day 1975, the 6-foot-11, 230-pound center had accomplished just about everything he could have in 12-plus seasons in the NBA. Seven All-Star games. Twice named to the NBA All-Defensive First Team. Voted to the league's All-Rookie First Team. The first of four players in NBA history to record a quadruple-double. And that's just a sampling. The one thing that Thurmond had yet to achieve in 11 seasons with the San Francisco/Golden State Warriors and one-plus seasons with the Chicago Bulls was an NBA Championship. Big number 42 had played in two Finals, both when he was with San Francisco, but was on the losing end in each of them. The trade to the Cavs was a homecoming of sorts for Thurmond. Born and raised in Akron, he was more than happy with the move.

"Things weren't going too well for me in Chicago," he said. "And my brother Ben, my parents, and my friends could come see me play."

Despite the Cavaliers' 6–10 record when he got to Cleveland, Thurmond thought the team had some talent.

"They had different guys who could score," he said, "but they needed a little bit of defensive toughness."

Although Thurmond could no doubt put the ball in the bucket throughout his career, he was known mainly for his awesome defense. He thrived in his role of backing up starting center Jim Chones.

"Thurmond was the first player who awakened Cavs fans—remember, Cleveland was still a young NBA city—as to how important playing defense is at that level," Mike Peticca said. "He was an intimidator. He was certainly past his prime, but he was still a game-changer as far as impacting the game defensively. And even on offense Thurmond was fun to watch because, boy, he set great picks. He was very consistent game in, game out that season. And, of course, as much as he helped with his playing, he was even more valuable with the intangibles. He certainly inspired the team and the fan base."

It didn't take long for the Cavaliers to heat up. After losing four of their first six games after the trade, they won seven straight games to inch above the .500 mark for the first time all season. From that point on, it was pretty much nip and tuck with the playoff-tested Washington Bullets in the Central Division. The Cavs wound up edging out the Bullets by one game, then beat them in seven hard-fought contests in an Eastern Conference Semifinal playoff series, three of Cleveland's victories coming in miraculous fashion. Unfortunately, in a practice session two days prior to the subsequent Conference Finals series against the Boston Celtics, Chones broke his right foot, forcing him out of action for the rest of the season and pushing Thurmond into more minutes than his 34-year-old body could handle. Thurmond and the Cavs put up a gallant effort against the veteran-laden Celtics, falling in six tough games. Thurmond took the defeat even harder than he did the two Finals he lost. In fact, he was in tears after Game 6.

"I knew that was pretty much the end," he said. "My gas was running out of my tank. The loss to Boston was a much more definitive loss than my Finals defeats. When I was a rookie, hey, I was just a rookie."

Thurmond was born on July 25, 1941, in Akron, not too far from where The Coliseum would be built 33 years later. He gained an interest in athletics at an early age. "I started out playing softball because my father used to play baseball," he said. "I was a pitcher and a pretty good one. Then, when I was in about sixth grade, I began playing basketball with my brother, who was almost two years older than me, at Spicer Grade School. There was a court in the back of the school that was on dirt, as a lot of courts were back then. I started playing organized basketball for Spicer when I was in seventh grade."

Not surprisingly, Nate was always the tallest kid in class. Even before he was of school age, his height made for good fodder. "When I'd hang around my father people would ask him why I wasn't in school, if was I sick," he laughed. "It was funny."

While he was leading his eighth-grade team to a phenomenal season, Thurmond practiced with Ben. "He wasn't very good," Nate said, "but he was good for me because he was kind of rough."

Big Brother was a good influence on Nate when he was with the Cavaliers, too, according to Bill Fitch. "Ben was such a great fan of Nate's when

Nate Thurmond. (Courtesy of AndersonsClevelandDesign.com)

he was with the Cavs," Fitch said, "that when people say, 'Geez coach, you did a great job with Thurmond,' I always give Ben the credit because he *was* really good for him."

Besides his height, Thurmond's ability aided his confidence. "I knew I was getting better," he said. However, Thurmond did not exactly draw salivating high school coaches to his games. "I was a late bloomer," he said.

Thurmond was already 6-foot-1 in his freshman year of 1955–56 at Akron Central (now Central-Hower) High School, where most of his teammates at Spicer also went. He played on the freshman team and then on the junior varsity squad the next year. He had been playing baseball at Central, too, but gave it up after his sophomore year on doctors' orders.

"They wanted me to slow down," he said. "They wanted me to play just one sport even though basketball and baseball were in different seasons. Because I was growing so fast, they felt it could've been dangerous. The summer between my sophomore and junior years I grew from 6-foot-4 to 6-foot-7."

Thurmond became a starter on the Wildcats' varsity team his junior year.

"I was losing some of the awkwardness from growing too fast," he said.

Both of Thurmond's parents were tall. His father Andrew was 6-foot-3, his mother Leala 5-foot-11. Ben was 6-foot-1. Nate's parents were both from the South—his father from Georgia, his mother from Alabama. His dad worked for Firestone Tire and Rubber Company. His mom, who played basketball in high school, was half-owner of a beauty salon.

"My mom and dad were supportive of me—but from afar," Nate said. "They didn't come to my games, but I didn't want them to. It was a strange situation. I thought I played better when they weren't there. I guess I got a little too nervous if they were there. And they were okay with that."

Central's teams in Thurmond's junior and senior years, coached by Joe Seigfreth, enjoyed great success. How could they not? In addition to Thurmond, who, believe it or not, played mainly forward, there was future NBA Hall of Famer Gus Johnson, who was the center most of the time.

"Gus was 6-foot-6, 240 all the way through high school," Thurmond said. "He was just so big and strong. He was the closest thing I knew back then to what LeBron [James] was in high school. I mean, this guy was really something. We also had a 6-foot-3 guard named Elijah Chatman, who came from Henry Grade School and who turned out to be my good friend. We practiced against each other every summer. We ended up playing in college together and were roommates all four years. Our point guard was about 5-foot-9 but really fast. We also had a guy by the name of Billy Sparks, a 6-foot-7, 260-pound football player, at the other forward spot. He was pretty agile. We had terrific teams."

Unfortunately, they were not good enough to advance to the Class AA (big schools at the time) state tournament in Columbus.

"We won the city championship but lost in the regionals both years," Thurmond recalled. "My junior year we really wanted to go to state and play against Jerry Lucas, who played for Middletown and was one year ahead of me, but we lost I think in the regional finals to Salem High School, whose star player was a guy named Lou Slaby, who was also a great football player and went on to play in the NFL. They pressed just as soon as we took the ball out, and we weren't expecting it. We only had that one terrific point guard, but they smothered him. The rest of us guys were big, but we didn't handle the ball well."

Thurmond was disappointed big-time that he and his teammates never advanced to the state tournament. "No question about it," he said.

By his senior year, Thurmond realized he could one day be something special. "I wasn't overly recruited," he said. "There were maybe six schools—Ohio State, some schools out West like Kansas that I wasn't even considering . . . and Bowling Green. Bowling Green was the hot pursuer. Elijah and I decided we were going to go to the same school, so we always went on recruiting visits together."

Thurmond accepted a full ride to play for Bowling Green State University. "Coach Seigfreth was a graduate of Bowling Green," he said, "and when we visited the campus I just thought it was the prettiest place I'd ever seen."

Thurmond was the starting center on the Falcons' freshman team. "If freshmen would've been allowed to play varsity," he said, "I would've played because, other than its star player, a great shooter named Jimmy Darrow, also from Akron, our varsity was weak."

Nate and his freshmen mates, including Chatman, also a starter, buried the varsity team in the annual varsity-freshmen game.

"That was expected," he said. "We had a really good freshman team. We killed 'em, absolutely annihilated 'em."

Looking back, however, Thurmond is glad the "no freshmen on varsity" rule was still in effect.

"I don't think I was ready for varsity competition yet," he admitted. "I was still slight of build and was still growing. There was no weight training back in those days, so they told you to eat more, whatever. Some of the football players lifted weights but not the basketball players. It was also an easier adjustment than it would've been had I gone to a school like Ohio State because the competition was much better at those bigger schools. I was still learning the game."

In order to improve his offensive skills, while at home in Akron the following summer Thurmond practiced against smaller players in pickup games after honing his shot, especially his outside shot, in the mornings by himself. "Eventually," he said, "I became a pretty good set shooter, with a range of about 12–15 feet."

Thurmond reiterated that, even by then, he was not the best ball handler. "That's why I felt more comfortable with my back to the basket at the center position," he said. "I was never comfortable driving to the hoop."

But with his improved shot, Thurmond's offensive game was starting to jell. "Plus, I wasn't growing as fast and my coordination was getting a little better," he said. "By the time we were sophomores, we were seasoned and ready to go. I was muscular but still a string bean and my offensive game was still raw, but I thought I was ready for the MAC [Mid-American Conference] because of my defensive skills. That was my strong suit and why I liked playing center better than forward. When you're in the middle guarding the basket . . . blocking shots . . . that's what I loved to do. I was also blessed with great lateral quickness."

Opponents were in awe of Thurmond and wanted no part of driving to the basket with him defending, including during his days in the NBA. "I've been told by NBA players after I retired that they'd say, 'Don't go to the hoop against Nate,'" he proudly stated.

"Nate the Great," as he was known by then, had grown to his peak height of 6-foot-11 by the start of his sophomore season in 1960–61. That year he averaged 17.8 points and 18.7 rebounds per game. As a junior, he hung up 15.7 points and 15.8 rebounds per game, leading Bowling Green to a 21–4 record and the MAC Championship. The Falcons lost by one point to Butler in the first round of the NCAA Tournament. The next year, Thurmond averaged 19.9 points and 16.7 boards per contest as BG went 19–8 and repeated as MAC champs. In the NCAA tourney, the Falcons defeated Notre Dame 77–72 in a first-round game but lost 70–67 to Illinois in a Mideast Regional Semifinal. Thurmond will never forget the game on February 16 that season in which he and his teammates pulled off a stunner, a 92–75 upset of visiting Loyola Chicago, the second-ranked team in the nation, which would go on to win the national title that year.

"It was unreal," he said. "It was nuts, absolutely nuts. The place was crazy. It was a shock. We thumped 'em pretty good. Their center was only about 6-foot-8, so I had no problem."

A physical education major with a minor in sociology, Thurmond thought he had a good shot at being chosen by the New York Knicks with the first overall pick in the 1963 NBA Draft. He wound up getting drafted by San Francisco with the third overall selection. It was a little surprising, considering the Warriors already had a guy by the name of Wilt Chamberlain in the middle.

"I don't know why they drafted me," laughed Thurmond, who admitted he was not exactly overjoyed. "I'd never been that far away from home either. I mean, that was way across the country. My parents also weren't too thrilled. They didn't want me to go that far away. But I didn't have any other options. You play where you're drafted, at least back then you did. I never considered doing anything else. I was going to play in the NBA. I could've been drafted by a team in Alaska and I was going to play."

In retrospect, Thurmond said it was a blessing in disguise that the Knicks passed over him. "I don't think personality-wise I'd have fit in in New York because the city was a little bit too big, too fast, for me at that time," he said.

Because the Warriors' offices were still in Philadelphia even though the team had relocated to San Francisco prior to the previous season, Thurmond flew to the City of Brotherly Love to meet with Warriors owner Eddie Gottlieb.

"Nobody picked me up at the airport," Thurmond said. "They told me to take a cab to some address on Broad Street. So I got down there, and Gottlieb, who was still living in Philly, offered me $12,000 for my rookie season with no signing bonus."

Remember, this was at a time when most professional athletes still earned the same kind of dough that the Average Joe made.

"I thought I was going to get $20,000 so I was really disheartened," recalled Thurmond, who, like all pro athletes at the time, acted as his own agent. "So I left with no contract and flew back to Ohio. When I got back to campus, my coach thought I was nuts. The mentality in those days was that you pretty much were paid what you were offered."

Eventually, Thurmond was able to squeeze $14,000, plus a $2,000 signing bonus, out of Gottlieb for a total of $16,000, which was $4,000 more than he was originally offered. "Four grand in those days was a lot of money," said Thurmond, who made $280,000 in his final year with the Cavaliers.

Thurmond's first impression of his new home in Northern California was positive. "I liked the weather," he said, "and it was a smaller city, at least compared to New York, so it was easier to navigate."

On the basketball court Thurmond made an immediate impact as a power forward for the Warriors, earning All-Rookie First-Team acclaim. He averaged seven points, but also 10.4 rebounds, per game, helping San Francisco to a 48–32 record and the Western Division Championship, a 17-game improvement from the year before. Thurmond and the Warriors defeated the St. Louis Hawks in seven games to advance to the NBA Finals against Boston, a franchise that had won six of the last seven, and was in the process of winning 11 of 13, NBA Championships. The Warriors lost four games to one.

"The coaches saw the potential in me," said Thurmond, who became good friends with Wayne Hightower, another power forward on the team, and point guard (and future Warriors head coach) Al Attles.

Now for The $64,000 Question: What was it like playing alongside the 7-foot-1, 275-pound "Wilt the Stilt," who averaged career *lows* at the time of 36.9 points and 22.3 rebounds per game that season?

"It was great because of who he was," Thurmond said. "And, in certain respects, it helped my game because it gave me the opportunity to deal with quicker forwards, which I could do. It also helped me get more confidence in my outside shot because they were double-teaming Wilt, so I got some open looks. There was a little pressure on me, too, because you felt you really let Wilt down when you missed. Wilt was also nice to me and very helpful, too. In practice I played center, so I had to guard Wilt, so I was learning as the season progressed even though I was out of position during games."

Asked what it was like going up against the great Celtics teams of that time, Thurmond said it was exhilarating and eventful. "I got to see up close the fierce rivalry between Wilt and Bill Russell," he said. "That was awesome, completely awesome. The intensity of each man's desire was incredible, it really was. I'd never seen anything like it. They didn't dislike each other and I saw the respect they had for each other, too. At Wilt's funeral years later Russell said of the two of them, 'We were joined at the hip.' And that was the way it was. If you talked about 'Russ' you talked about Wilt, if you talked about Wilt you talked about Russ because they were complete opposites as far as their games were concerned. Russ was blessed with a lot of firepower. He had [Bob] Cousy, he had [John] Havlicek, he had [Tom] Heinsohn, he had Sam Jones . . . so he could solely concentrate on defense. Wilt was on some teams where there were no other Top 50 players, so he was more offensive-oriented. I made my reputation because I could defend Wilt and Kareem [Abdul-Jabbar]. Muhammad [Ali] made his reputation because he had a great Joe Frazier to fight against. That's how reputations are made, so Wilt and Russ were . . . it was just like, 'Wow, I've got to outdo you' and 'No you're not,' that type of thing."

Thurmond began putting up Hall of Fame numbers himself in his second season of 1964–65. Maybe not Chamberlain numbers—who did?—but definitely Hall of Fame numbers. In fact, from the '64–65 season all the way through 1972–73, Thurmond never averaged fewer than 16.3 points per game, and other than one season, never averaged fewer than 16.1 rebounds per contest. His finest season came in 1967–68 when he hung up 20.5 points and 22 rebounds per game. Thurmond's specialty was defense, and blocked shots were not even recognized as an official NBA statistic until 1973–74 when he began his decline from his prime years.

Thurmond and the Warriors won only 17 games in 1964–65, a season in which Chamberlain was traded to the Philadelphia 76ers at the All-Star break. With Thurmond now at center and hotshot Rick Barry, the second overall pick in the 1965 NBA Draft, now in the fold as small forward, the Warriors improved to 35–45 the next season. By the time the 1966–67 season—Bill Sharman's first as head coach, replacing Alex Hannum—began, the Warriors were ready to make a run at a championship again. With Thurmond putting up his usual outstanding numbers and Barry averaging a career-high 35.6 points per game, they finished with a 44–37 record, not eye-popping by any means but enough to win the weak Western Division. They defeated the Los Angeles Lakers three games to none and then the St. Louis Hawks four games to two to advance to the championship round for the first time since Thurmond's rookie season. San Francisco's opponent in the Finals? None other than old buddy Chamberlain and the Sixers, who finished 68–13—the NBA's best record ever up to that point—during the regular season. The Warriors lost in six games.

"We had a really good team," Thurmond said. "We played them tough. There were a couple calls that went their way. Most people think that was the greatest team Philly ever assembled. Besides Wilt, they had Hal Greer, Chet Walker, and Billy Cunningham, all future Hall of Famers. We were the youngest team ever to reach the Finals at that particular time. Then Rick left for the ABA, so that put a crimp into what we had going. Our owner, Franklin Mieuli, who'd replaced Gottlieb soon after I got to San Francisco my rookie year, was very, very angry about it. I was, too. I thought Rick messed up a good thing for our team because we were young, we were good, and we were going to get better."

The Warriors lost in the Western Division Finals the next season and in the first round the season after that before plummeting to a 30–52 record in 1969–70.

"We were just not as good without Rick," said Thurmond.

The Warriors returned to the postseason in 1970–71 and '71–72 but failed to win a playoff series again until 1972–73 when Barry returned to the club, which by this time was known as the Golden State Warriors. Golden State reached the Western Conference Finals that year, falling to the Lakers four games to one. Thurmond was in for quite a shock after the following season when he was traded to Chicago.

"They felt I was at the end of my career," he said.

Thurmond was the Bulls' starting center for the first few months of 1974–75 before giving way to the younger Tom Boerwinkle. That year, the Bulls won the Midwest Division with a 47–35 record and advanced to the Western Conference Finals. Their opponent? Golden State.

"We lost the series in seven games but we had a chance to win," Thurmond said. "We blew a 16-point lead in one game and something crazy happened in another. Those were two games that we kind of let slip out of our grasp. I played horribly in that series. We would've won if I'd have played decently. No question that was on me."

Thurmond admitted being relegated to backup status was a blow to his ego. "I was still able to contribute," he said, "but, to tell you the truth, I didn't fit in with Chicago's offensive system, which was basically to get the ball into our forwards. Sometimes a team gets you, but they don't change their system at all to make your skills better."

After he was traded to the Cavaliers and following the Miracle of Richfield season, Thurmond, who had battled the injury bug—including two operations on his right knee while with the Warriors—returned for perhaps one last hurrah. Unfortunately, he tore cartilage in his left knee more than halfway through the 1976–77 campaign, requiring yet another surgery.

"After I rehabbed," he laughed, "that was it because . . . I will never forget this. This is not a slam on this player, but Coach Fitch had me working out with John Lambert, one of our backup forwards. I couldn't stop him. I knew it was time to go."

Although he made a token appearance in the Cavs' '77 Game 2 first-round playoff win over Washington, Thurmond hung up the sneakers after 13-and-a-half seasons. He did color commentary for local televised Cavaliers broadcasts for a season before settling in San Francisco—"I didn't like the Ohio winters," he said—and taking it easy for a couple of years. He then took a job in community relations with the Warriors, a position he still holds but, since 2008, only on a part-time basis. Thurmond was a busy man; in 1990 he opened a restaurant near downtown San Francisco called "Big Nate's," which specialized in barbecue.

"My partner in owning the restaurant, who left after a few years, and I were sitting around talking," Thurmond recalled. "My mom had given me a great barbecue sauce recipe and we were noticing how many Domino's Pizza cars we saw with the Domino thing on top of them. So we said, 'These guys deliver all over the city, wow! Why don't we try to deliver barbecued food? It's deliverable. If it's good barbecued food, it doesn't have to be piping hot.'"

That concept is what turned Big Nate's into a rousing success that won numerous awards. "It kept me open for 20 years," said a proud Thurmond.

Big Nate's top sellers were barbecued beef, Memphis pork, ribs, and chicken. "Our main focus was delivery and takeout, but we also had seats for 20," said Thurmond, whose son Adam helped run the restaurant as its manager for nine years. "Having my name as part of the name of the restaurant was very important to its success, of course. I'd lived here a long time and knew a lot of people."

Thurmond did not rely solely on his celebrated surname, however. "As a business person," he said, "I believed that you also had to have consistently good food. And our food was consistently good, and the reason was that I was blessed in that I had several workers who were there a long time. That's unbelievable in a small business." Thurmond sold the restaurant in 2010. He had actually owned a soul food establishment, called "The Beginning," also in San Francisco, in the 1970s. "San Francisco is certainly a restaurant town," he said. "Restaurants close every day, but we at Big Nate's were able to stick it out."

Nate also co-hosts pregame and postgame shows on the local ABC affiliate for each game of the NBA Finals and one conference championship game. "It's just enough to keep my mug in front of the TV periodically," he laughed.

These days, Thurmond enjoys a tranquil existence in San Francisco with his wife of 23 years, Marci. On the weekends, the two of them enjoy taking drives to different parts of California.

"We get in the car, we go north, we go south, whatever," said Nate, who hates flying. "We just take off with no set agenda. There are all kinds of interesting little towns in this state. We also enjoy music and eating at different restaurants."

Thurmond said his father was extremely influential to him when it came to his personal life. "He taught me a lot of things that are still valuable today, there's no question about it, like my modesty," he said. "You let other people talk about you, you don't talk about yourself. He taught me how to be a gentleman. The only thing that he tried to teach me that I didn't learn was how to save money. He was great at that, I'm not. That's why I worked until I was almost 70!"

As for the most influential person on him professionally, Thurmond said it was Chamberlain and later, Magic Johnson. "Wilt knew how to make money," he said. "In later years I became enamored with Magic, too, what he's done as a businessman. I admire him so much, he'll never know. He just stands out. I mean, he's all over the country with different businesses that are so successful. Here's a guy who's worth over half a billion dollars, and he didn't make what these guys are making today."

Asked if he ever considered venturing into the coaching profession, Thurmond laughed. "No way," he said. "I could *play* the game, but I couldn't explain it. I couldn't draw up a play."

Fitch thought the world of his veteran big man. "Nate was a leader and set a great example for the younger players," he said. "Not once did he say, 'I'm too tired.' He was a hell of a guy."

"It wasn't necessarily what Nate did on the court," Les Levine said. "You could argue whether he deserved to have his number retired by the Cavaliers [Thurmond's number 42 is retired], but you couldn't argue that he was a Hall of Famer who still had quite a presence when he got to the Cavs."

Tom Melody recalled just how big of a presence Thurmond was off the court. "Nate would periodically come into the newsroom and come over to the sports department," he said. "He might've come down for an interview or there might've been something that he was helping out with. Of course, this was when we still had typewriters and the room was always just clickety-clack, clickety-clack. And Nate would come through the door, and as he'd walk through the room and as more people saw him, all the typewriters would just stop. It was like this was the biggest individual they'd ever seen or something. And, by the time he'd get over to sports, the newsroom would just be silent and everybody would be staring at him. But he'd take it in stride, he'd never say anything about it."

Voted in 1996 as one of the 50 Greatest Players in NBA History and a 1985 inductee to the Naismith Memorial Basketball Hall of Fame, Thurmond, whose number 42 is also retired by the Warriors, recalled a moment from the night of April 10, 1973, that he will never forget.

"I was with Golden State," he said. "We beat Milwaukee with Kareem—a young Kareem—in a six-game playoff series. The series was tied 2–2 and we beat them in Game 5 in Milwaukee. Kareem had averaged more than 30 points per game that year, and I held him to 19 and his lowest shooting percentage—like 42 or something—in that fifth game. When I was taken out of the game, the fans in Milwaukee gave me a standing ovation. At first, I didn't know what was happening, thinking, 'Why are they standing up?' That was the highest honor for me as a player on an individual basis."

"Nate was exactly the same player in the pros as he was in high school, only a lot better," said Sheldon Ocker. "He never, or rarely, looked to score, he never took a shot out of his range, and he never took a bad shot. His first thoughts were playing defense and rebounding. Nate was one of the best there ever was in defending the post."

Still, many NBA fans think of Abdul-Jabbar, Chamberlain, and Russell when it comes to the greatest centers of all time. It is unfortunate that Thurmond, who not surprisingly ranks those three players as the toughest he ever faced, is all too often left off that list. "Nate could compete with all of them toe-to-toe," Chones said.

Thurmond mentioned a few other Hall of Famers who were tough competitors. "Dave Cowens," he said, "was a great all-around player, tough on the boards, played both ends of the court. Willis Reed . . . same thing, sweet hook shot, could face up. Bob McAdoo . . . if you didn't watch out, he'd put up 45 on you. Wes Unseld . . . he'd bounce you around the gym with his body. They were all tough."

Asked if those legendary players would say the same of him, Thurmond paused before responding.

"I hope so," he said.

20 | Campy Russell

The Cavaliers of the mid- to late-1970s had some great shooters. Bingo Smith. Dick Snyder. Austin Carr. None of them, however, had a turnaround jump shot quite like Campy Russell's. There were times that Russell's legendary turnaround came from as far as 25 feet from the basket. It was remarkable.

"It was also textbook perfect," said Les Levine. "Sometimes you wondered how it went in because so many things had to happen with Campy's technique, except it happened so often that you realized it wasn't by chance."

Considered by many Cavs fans to be one of the greatest shooters in team history, Russell takes issue with that, in a sense. He never thought he was a good shooter per se like Smith, Snyder, and Carr. He considered himself more of a scorer than a shooter because of his ability to drive to the hoop and get to the foul line. Russell, indeed, led the Cavaliers in free-throw attempts every season from 1975–76 to '78–79.

Born Michael Russell on January 12, 1952, in Jackson, Tennessee, Campy was 4 years old when his family moved to Pontiac, Michigan. The fourth youngest of 10 children, he was raised in a neighborhood full of youngsters, with playgrounds everywhere. He took part in all the sports—baseball, basketball, football . . . even horseshoes! Russell's two brothers, Frank and Walker, and one of his sisters were very good basketball players. In fact, Frank and Walker went on to play in the NBA. Frank, Campy's older brother, was a big influence on him when it came to getting involved in athletics, especially basketball.

Russell, who was 6-foot-8, 215 pounds while with the Cavs, came from a family with tall genes. Walker was 6-foot-5, Frank was 6-foot-3, his dad was 6-foot-1, and his mom was 5-foot-9. His sisters were tall, too, as was one of his grandmothers. His father, who lived to be 98 years old, was such a huge baseball fan that he named Campy, whose middle name is Campanella, after Brooklyn Dodgers Hall of Fame catcher Roy Campanella.

Russell began playing organized basketball in the sixth grade, but it wasn't until the following summer that he became hooked on hoops. That was when he attended the All-Pro Basketball Camp in the Poconos run by Dave Bing, a camp that through the years has attracted the likes of Sam Bowie, Moses Malone, and David Blatt as campers and the likes of Wes Unseld and Sam Jones as lecturers. Because the emphasis at the camp was on being able to be a complete player, Russell became a much better ball handler, passer, and shooter. His time at the camp fine-tuned his game and provided him with a better understanding of how to play the sport. He became a camp counselor there in the summer before ninth grade, lecturing and teaching all the way until the early part of his NBA career.

When he arrived at Central High School, which had been a basketball powerhouse for years and continued to be all the way up until it closed in 2009, Russell, who had played center in junior high due to his size, was more than ready for what lay ahead. Both of his brothers had starred at Central, so he wanted to carry on the fine family tradition there. He continued to play center, but it was more of a hybrid kind of thing. He was given many tasks, including bringing the ball up on the break, because he had those different skill sets.

Russell was the Chiefs' starting center from 10th through 12th grade. He also ran track and was the state high jump champ as a junior. He played football through his sophomore year until the basketball coach told him to quit. When he was a sophomore, Russell helped Central advance to the Class A (big schools) state tournament quarterfinals. The next year, the team was state runner-up, and in his senior year it fell in the quarters again. Russell was Central's leading scorer and rebounder all three seasons. In fact, he amassed in the vicinity of 46 points in one game, breaking Frank's school record by four points or so. He was First-Team All-State all three years and was a Parade All-American his senior year.

By this time, Russell was fully grown. He was *thinking* big, too—as in the NBA. But first things first: He was being pursued by most of the prominent colleges across the country. There were those who said, at the time, that Russell was the best high school player in the nation. That was likely due, in large part, to his performances in various all-star games, including the revered Dapper Dan Roundball Classic in Pittsburgh. It came down to the University of Michigan and Michigan State University. Russell accepted a full scholarship to play at Michigan, some 50 miles from Pontiac, because he liked the school and he wanted his parents and friends to be able to go watch him play.

Russell starred as a power forward on the Wolverines' freshman team in 1971–72, which was undefeated in some 10 games and was the second-ranked freshman team in the nation behind only the David Thompson–led North Carolina State Wolfpack. By his sophomore year, although he still brought the ball up the court at times, Russell was becoming more of a true forward. That season, he started and averaged 18.4 points and 9.6 rebounds per game for a Michigan team that failed to live up to its preseason billing and finished just 13–11. Russell, though, was getting rave reviews as evidenced by his adorning the cover of *Sports Illustrated* early that season. He could have left Michigan for the ABA but chose not to. Although he felt he was ready from a talent standpoint, he did not believe he was prepared mentally and physically.

The next year, Russell amassed a team-leading 23.7 points and 11.1 rebounds per contest, leading Michigan to a 22–5 record and the Big Ten title that was not clinched until the Wolverines defeated Indiana in a tiebreaker playoff. He and his teammates upset third-ranked Notre Dame 77–68 in an NCAA Tournament Mideast Regional Semifinal before bowing out of the tourney with a 72–70 defeat to a Marquette team led by future NBA great Maurice Lucas.

Russell left Michigan for the NBA after his junior year. He was chosen by the Cavaliers in the first round—the eighth overall pick—of the 1974 NBA Draft. He was surprised that Cleveland drafted him and was also somewhat disappointed due to the fact that the Cavs were not exactly an established franchise. In the '74 ABA Draft, he *was* drafted by an established franchise—the defending champion, and Julius Erving–led, New York Nets. He opted to sign with Cleveland, however, due to the fact that the ABA was on shaky ground.

Russell spent his rookie season of 1974–75 frustrated with his lack of playing time at his new position of small forward while watching his team miss the playoffs by one game. Bill Fitch brought him along more slowly than he would have liked due to the presence of veterans Smith and Fred Foster. Russell felt he was ready to play from the very start. Looking back, though, he agreed that Fitch did the right thing because it gave him a chance to acclimate himself to the NBA at a slower pace, and it helped him diminish his development curve in terms of being ready to play when his number was called.

In his second season, the Miracle of Richfield year, Russell became a key cog off the bench, averaging 15 points and 4.2 rebounds per game. He averaged a team-leading 16.5 points and six rebounds per game in 1976–77 and then a team-best 19.4 points and 6.4 boards per contest the next season, both years in which the Cavaliers won 43 games but lost in the first round of the playoffs, the latter in which he finally cracked the starting lineup. In 1978–79, for a Cavs team that dropped to 30–52, Russell amassed a team-leading 21.9 points, 6.8 rebounds, and 4.7 assists per game, all career highs, which resulted in his lone All-Star Game appearance. The next season, he was having a fabulous year—18.2 points and 5.5 boards per contest—when halfway through the schedule he suffered a season-ending injury, which likely cost the team a playoff berth.

Two weeks before the start of the 1980–81 season Russell was traded to the Kansas City Kings, but as a result of a three-team deal, wound up with the New York Knicks, with whom he had two solid seasons. He retired and then tore his right ACL while working out during the summer of 1982. He had surgery, then sat out the next two seasons before attempting a comeback. He was traded backs to the Cavaliers, with whom he spent the first week-and-a-half of 1984–85 before being waived. After a stint with the CBA's Detroit Spirits that season, he called it quits.

Russell stayed in the "Motor City" and ventured into the steel business. He spent 18 years in sales with General Motors, Ford, and Chrysler. In the early 2000s, he accepted the head-coaching position at a local community college but passed on the opportunity when he noticed on the Cavaliers' website that an outer market sales position with the team was open. He contacted the Cavs and got the job. He became their director of alumni relations in 2005. The year before, he joined the Cavs' local television broadcast booth as an analyst for pregame, halftime, and postgame shows. Russell lives in Cleveland with his wife Robyn. The couple has five children, daughters Oyin, Mandisa, Saki, and Allex, and son Michael II, and 11 grandchildren. Russell enjoys playing golf during the offseason.

A sports management and communications major who returned to the University of Michigan in 1999–2000 to earn his degree, Russell was inducted into the school's Hall of Honor in 2002. He was one of the most gifted players in Cavaliers history.

"Campy was an unbridled talent, a raw talent," said Nate Thurmond. "He had all kinds of offensive weapons—he could shoot from the outside, he could go to the hole . . . I don't think he knew how good he was. I'd have loved to see Campy be a guy who never left the gym. He would've been one of the best players of that era."

"Campy," Mike Peticca added, "had maybe as versatile a set of skills as any player the Cavs had until LeBron James. Probably in an emergency he could've even played point guard. What a terrific passer, and he had so many different ways he could score.

"He was so much fun to watch from a fan's standpoint."

21 | Lambert, Luke, and the Rest

John Lambert

His nickname may have been "Hollywood" due to his movie-star looks, but John Lambert, at least on the basketball court, was anything *but* glitz and glamour. A first-round pick—the 15th selection overall—by the Cavaliers out of the University of Southern California in the 1975 NBA Draft, the 6-foot-10, 225-pound Lambert, a backup power forward for the Cavs, could get down and dirty and snag a clutch rebound when needed. He also could put the ball in the bucket. His career high of 18 points came against the Washington Bullets on January 22, 1980. Lambert was also mentally tough.

"John was one of those guys who'd go toe-to-toe with Bill Fitch verbally, even as a rookie," Dick Snyder said. "Most guys wouldn't do that. They'd be a little too intimidated."

Born on January 14, 1953, in Berkeley, California, Lambert graduated from Berkeley High School in 1971 before heading down Interstate 5 to Southern California. After playing on the freshman team, Lambert helped the Trojans to 18–10, 24–5, and 18–8 records, respectively, and a pair of runner-up finishes in the PAC-8. He led his team both with 6.9 rebounds per game his junior year and 10.2 boards per contest his senior year. He also averaged 14.2 points per game as a senior.

"John was raw but he understood the game," said Nate Thurmond. "He kept alert as far as how hard he practiced, and he never complained about not playing. When somebody got into foul trouble, he'd go in there and do his thing. And when his jump shot was falling from the corner, he really helped us in a few games."

John Lambert (*left*) and Bill Fitch during a preseason practice session, September 1975. (The Cleveland Press Collection, Michael Schwartz Library, Cleveland State University)

"John was probably the most-improved player on the team from beginning to end during his rookie season," Fitch said. "He learned a lot from the guys he played with. And he had the range and the length."

Snyder believes things might have been different for Lambert while he was with the Cavaliers had he been in the right place at the right time. "It's really a shame because John could've been a solid player," he said. "Take when Jim [Chones] got hurt before the Boston playoff series in '76 . . . if that had happened another year or two down the line, I think we might've beaten the Celtics just with Nate and John. John hadn't gotten that much playing time that year, and all of a sudden he was thrust into a situation where he had to play some significant minutes. That was tough for him."

Lambert proved Snyder prophetic with his performance in the spring of 1981 as a member of the Kansas City Kings. He had signed with the Kings as a free agent on the day after the previous Christmas after having been waived by the Cavs seven days earlier.

"That Kings team," Mike Peticca said, "made a nice run in the playoffs, and John was a valuable contributor on those teams that had Scott Wedman and Otis Birdsong. He had a little stretch where he really helped them."

Lambert indeed scored his career playoff high of 16 points, helping Kansas City to an 88–79 victory over Houston in Game 2 of the Western Conference Finals on April 22, 1981. "What's funny," continued Peticca, "is that maybe in today's game John would be developed into a stretch four."

Lambert finished his NBA career in 1982 with the San Antonio Spurs, to whom he was traded in February of that year. He played a season in Italy and then retired.

Lambert was a likeable guy.

"You really couldn't not like John because he was always smiling and joking," Snyder said.

"One thing about Lambert, he could talk black and he could talk white," Joe Tait laughed. "It was fun to listen to him when he got into discussions with the black players because he could talk just like they did. And then he'd turn right around and talk like a college professor to the white players."

"I remember eating lunch with John at a hotel on the road one time," recalled Sheldon Ocker. "He'd lose weight during the season. He couldn't keep weight on. So he'd order two lunches. He'd just tell the waiter, 'Give me two of these, two of these, and two of these.'"

Tait likened Lambert to the movie *The Picture of Dorian Gray*.

"In essence," he said, "it was about a man who never aged and yet had a painting of himself in the attic of his home, and the painting was aging all the time. At the end, the painting was decrepit and disgusting but he never changed. And that's the way it was with John Lambert."

With his good looks and high metabolism, had he selected a different career path post-basketball, instead of the banking business, perhaps Lambert, not Sylvester Stallone, would have portrayed the iconic "Rambo" character in the immensely successful *First Blood/Rambo* film series, the first of which was released some five months after Lambert retired.

Rambo's first name in those films? None other than . . . John.

Rowland Garrett

Rowland Garrett's first three seasons in the NBA were pretty quiet for him individually. Although he was a member of a Chicago Bulls team that was a perennial title contender, he was a benchwarmer for the most part. That was understandable because veteran Chet Walker, a future Hall of Famer, was the Bulls' starter at Garrett's position of small forward.

When Walker retired after the 1974–75 season, Garrett, a fifth-round draft pick of the Bulls in 1972 out of Florida State University, still found himself in the far reaches on the depth chart. Injuries sustained by others, though, propelled him to a more meaningful role early in the 1975–76 season. He took full advantage of it, too. His best game was on October 28 when he scored 22 points and had 14 rebounds in a 101–90 victory over the Seattle SuperSonics. Garrett also had 22- and 17-point nights against Philadelphia and a pair of 16-point outings against Boston and Detroit. Then, on Thanksgiving Day, two days after he scored 10 points in a loss to the Cavaliers, the 6-foot-6, 210-pound Garrett was traded to those same Cavs in a deal that also brought Nate Thurmond to Cleveland.

"I was starting to come along and play well, then suddenly I got traded," he said. "I couldn't understand it."

Garrett was born on July 16, 1950, in Canton, Mississippi, a town of about 15,000 people. "I was kind of an awkward little kid," he said. "I'd go to the gym and watch guys play basketball. I couldn't hold a basketball because my hands were too little, so I started playing with a rolled up sock and a baseball." By the time he was in the sixth grade, Garrett could hold the rock. There were two high schools in Canton—an all-white school and Rogers High, the all-black school that Garrett attended.

"I went out for football my freshman year," he said. "I was going to be a tight end. I could chase the ball pretty good, but the basketball coach kind of ran me out of there. He told me, 'Your future is in basketball.'"

Garrett started on the junior varsity team as a freshman and on the varsity squad his last three years.

"I played forward, I played center . . . I played everywhere," he said.

As a senior, Garrett led Rogers to the big-school state championship game, which it lost by one point. That year, he averaged in the absurd vicinity of both a team-leading 35 points and 25 rebounds per game.

"I even averaged about nine dunks a game," he laughed. "I was also blocking everything."

Garrett was named First-Team All-State and First-Team All-American by *Scholastic Magazine*. Some 100 schools, including the powerhouse UCLA program, recruited him.

"I didn't want to go too far away," he said, "and Florida State University was only about 450 miles from home. I also liked the school and all the guys."

Garrett accepted a full ride and started at small forward on FSU's freshman team, which lost no more than a couple of games, and started at the same position his last three years. He and the Seminoles finished 23–3 his sophomore year and 17–9 his junior year. He averaged 12.5 points and 8.2 rebounds per game in the latter.

As a senior in 1971–72, Garrett's 13.1 points and 7.9 rebounds per contest helped Florida State to a 28–5 record and just its second appearance in the NCAA Tournament. FSU won the program's first-ever tourney game by beating Eastern Kentucky, then defeated Minnesota and Kentucky, respectively, to advance to the Final Four. The Cinderella Seminoles upset the Bob McAdoo–led North Carolina Tar Heels 79–75 in the semifinals. Their opponent in the championship game? None other than UCLA, the giant on the top of the mountain that seemingly nobody could knock off. The Bruins, led by future NBA Hall of Famers Bill Walton and Jamaal Wilkes, and also future NBAer Henry Bibby, were in the midst of a record 88-game winning streak and 10 national titles in 12 years.

"I ended up having to guard Walton," Garrett said, "because I think our center fouled out. We had them down 17–5. We had two guards who no one in the world could press and they came out and tried to press us."

UCLA came back to win 81–76.

"It wasn't Walton who beat us, though," said Garrett. "It was Wilkes and Bibby. Those were the guys who really beat us."

Garrett, who majored in art education, had always wanted to play in the NBA but realized it was a long shot. "I just did the best I could and worked as hard as I could. I never let up," he said.

After getting traded to the Cavaliers, Garrett spent the remainder of the 1975–76 season and part of the '76–77 campaign as a backup. He did have some good games, though, including a 15-point outing against Milwaukee on January 24, 1976.

"Rowland could run the floor. He was like a deer, and he took pride in that," Thurmond said. "He got a lot of leak-out baskets, he would get some

Rowland Garrett goes for two against Atlanta during the Miracle of Richfield season. (Courtesy of AndersonsClevelandDesign.com)

boards for you, and he could play a little bit of 'D.' He wasn't necessarily a great shooter but certainly a finisher."

"He was a good pickup," said Bill Fitch. "He was a good enough small forward that defensively he probably had a lot to do with how good Campy [Russell] got because he wanted that job, and Campy wanted it, so he pushed Campy. If something had happened up front in terms of an injury, I wouldn't have been afraid to play Rowland. He did a good job in practice and he was good enough that he kept his minutes whenever I could put him in, which kept [Bingo] Smith and Russell fresh."

"Rowland was a nice player," Dick Snyder said. "He just didn't get the opportunity to play much with the Cavaliers."

Garrett was traded to the Bucks less than halfway through the 1976–77 season but saw little playing time and was waived prior to the next season. After taking a year off, he played in Italy for two years before retiring. He returned to Mississippi and started a chemical manufacturing company, GNG Enterprises, which is still going strong today. He and his wife of 27 years, Esther, live in Jackson, some 30 miles from Canton. Garrett has four grown children, two with Esther and two from a previous marriage, and three grandchildren. He continued to play hoops, competing in city and AAU leagues for years before venturing into the world of karate, specifically tae kwon do. He is a fifth-degree black belt with a pair of state championships to his credit.

Garrett may not have mastered the NBA, but he did have his moments. His remarkable performance against the Sonics in his final season with the Bulls may have been his finest game statistically as a pro, but his most memorable moment, also as a Bull, came when he had an encounter with the one and only Kareem Abdul-Jabbar.

"I was running down the floor pretty fast on the break," he said, "and Kareem was under the basket. I kind of caught him by surprise and dunked on him.

"I really enjoyed that."

Luke Witte

It is a crying shame that when many longtime basketball fans think of former Cavalier Luke Witte, the first thing that comes to mind is the infamous melee between Witte's Ohio State Buckeyes and the Minnesota Golden Gophers that occurred in Minneapolis on the evening of January 25, 1972, resulting in a Buckeyes forfeit victory. It is a shame because Witte, OSU's starting center that night, was a fabulous college basketball player. As a result of the brouhaha, he had 27 stitches to his face. Two of his teammates also wound up in the hospital.

"I had a concussion and a scratched cornea on my right eye, too," Witte said. "I was also kicked in the groin."

Most observers opine that Witte, who remarkably missed just one game due to his injuries, was never the same after the incident, which also included a large dose of Golden Gopher, and Witte's future Cavs teammate, Jim Brewer. Witte's statistics, however, seem to prove otherwise. He finished that 1971–72 season, his junior year, averaging 17 points and a team-leading 12.6 rebounds per game as Ohio State finished 18–6 and in second place in the Big Ten. There was a falloff, but not a huge one, in his senior year, when he averaged 13.7 points and a team-best 8.3 rebounds per contest as the Buckeyes finished 14–10 and in a tie for third place in the conference.

After having started at center, where he would remain for the rest of his career, on Ohio State's undefeated freshman team in 1969–70, Witte averaged 18.9 points and a team-high 12.7 rebounds per game his sophomore year, leading the Buckeyes to a 20–6 record, the Big Ten title, and advancement to the Mideast Regional Final of the NCAA Tournament, where they lost 81–78 to Western Kentucky.

Witte was born on October 19, 1950, in Philadelphia. He did not stay there very long, though. "My father was a pastor and we moved around a lot," he said, noting West Philadelphia; Princeton, New Jersey; and Greenville, South Carolina, as places in which he lived. "My parents divorced—my dad had an affair—and that kind of disrupted the family and everything else for a while. So when I was 12 I went and moved in with my oldest brother Wylan, who was 13 years older than me, and his wife on their farm in Marlboro, Ohio, just outside of Alliance. The town had 350 whole people! I'd spent some time up there before, and the idea of just being able to work on the farm . . . that was really a blessing. I'm an introvert by nature, and with the divorce of my parents my desire was to just hide. My salvation at that point in my life was basketball because I was still growing. I was a big kid. I practiced in the barn. That's what I did."

Witte's mother eventually moved to Marlboro, as did his other brother, who was seven years his senior.

"My mom," he said, "built a house not far from where I'd been living and I moved in with her when I was about 15."

As a youngster Witte played baseball and football in addition to basketball.

"I played all the typical big-guy positions," he said, "first base in baseball, tight end in football, and of course, center in basketball. I loved basketball.

It was my favorite by far and it was the one I was best at. I can't remember my seventh- and eighth-grade teams losing more than one or two games combined. I was about 6-foot-4 by then and still growing."

By the time he was a freshman at Marlington High School, Witte had grown to about 6-foot-6.

"I was playing football my freshman year and I hurt my back," he said. "While I was standing on the sidelines during practice, the varsity basketball coach came up to me, put his hand on my back, and said while laughing, 'Why don't you play something you're good at?' That was the last time I played organized football. I wasn't very good at baseball either and eventually gave that up, too. I was pretty good in the field, but at the plate I had a large strike zone."

Witte started at center, where he would remain for the rest of his basketball career, on the Dukes' freshman team. By the time he was a sophomore, he was nearly full grown at 6-foot-11 and ⅜.

"My coaches never let me dribble," he laughed. "We were Class AA [big schools] then but just barely. A team by the name of Canton McKinley, with a guy named Nick Weatherspoon, seemed to be a problem for us. They beat us in the district tournament all three years, the last two in the finals."

A First-Team All-Ohioan and an All-American his senior year, Witte's desire was to play at the next level for the University of Iowa. "My family is originally from Iowa," he said, "so I thought it'd be really neat to have the opportunity to play there. But Iowa never recruited me!"

Witte was sought after by 200–300 schools across the country, including Ohio State University, the University of North Carolina, Duke University, and UCLA, a program that was in the midst of winning 10 national championships in 12 years.

"UCLA," he laughed, "seemed to have a few guys out there who I probably wouldn't have beaten out."

It came down to Ohio State and North Carolina.

"North Carolina had never had a good center come out of there," Witte said. "They ran the four-corner offense. That leaves *somebody* out. At least [Ohio State head coach] Fred [Taylor] had the ability and desire—he was a big man himself—to get the ball inside. So that was one reason I chose Ohio State. The main reason, though, was so my mom could watch me play."

Witte received a full ride to play at Ohio State, a school that was known for more than just its renowned Woody Hayes–led football program. The basketball Buckeyes had a fine tradition themselves. In fact, they had reached the NCAA Tournament Final Four in 1968, and, led by future NBA Hall of Famers Jerry Lucas and John Havlicek, had appeared in three straight National Championship games from 1960–62, winning the school's only title in 1960.

Witte, an alternate on the 1972 U.S. Summer Olympic team that lost to the Soviet Union in the controversial gold medal game, majored in journalism. Unlike many graduating college players the following spring, it was not life or death for him when it came to making it to the NBA.

"It wasn't like, 'If I don't make it big time, or to the NBA, my life is over.' I never thought those kinds of things," he said. "I don't think I had some of the incentive to make it to the NBA that a lot of other players did."

The 7-foot, 235-pound Witte was chosen by the Cavaliers in the fourth round of the 1973 NBA Draft. He was also selected by the San Antonio Spurs in the ABA Draft. A conversation he had with Havlicek at a Columbus barber shop helped him decide whether to go to Cleveland or San Antonio.

"John asked me what I was going to do and I said, 'I think I'm going with the Spurs,'" Witte recalled. "And he said, 'I wouldn't do that.' And I said, 'Why?' He said, 'Well, the ABA's going to go defunct, and we're [the NBA] going to bring in some of its teams.' He really discouraged me from going to the ABA. Then I got a phone call from my roommate. He said that Cleveland had just phoned me. So I called the Cavs from the barber shop! It turned out their offer was a little bit better than San Antonio's anyway. I didn't have an agent so I said, 'I'll take it.' Bill Fitch was Wylan's coach when he was at Coe College, so I knew Bill when I was like 7 or 8 years old."

Witte backed up Steve Patterson in his rookie year of 1973–74. He had quite a month of January that season, scoring in double figures seven times, topped by a career-high 17-point performance against Los Angeles on the 22nd. He backed up Jim Chones in 1974–75 and Chones and Nate Thurmond in the Miracle of Richfield season. How did Witte handle going from All-Everything in high school and a terrific college career to sitting on the bench in the pros? Ever the philosopher, Witte explained: "There's a natural progression, there's a learning curve. I was sitting on the sidelines waiting for my break to happen, waiting for bigger things to come along. So you're always anticipating, you're always thinking, 'When I get my chance I'm going to do the best I can.' Every time you get into a game, you want to make sure that you hold your own whatever the situation. And so I tried my very best to do that. I can remember Bill saying, 'You played 10 minutes in there and you only had one foul! Bill could be pretty hard on you, but I'd have to say he treated me honestly and fairly all the way through my career."

Luke Witte against the Hawks with Jimmy Rodgers (*left*) and Charlie Strasser in the background, April 4, 1976. (The Cleveland Press Collection, Michael Schwartz Library, Cleveland State University)

"Luke was a big guy, he took up space in the middle," Thurmond said. "He had some low-post abilities," added Mike Peticca.

Witte was one of the hardest workers on the Cavs. "We used to have horrific road trips," he said, "like seven-, eight-day trips . . . to the West Coast . . . and sometimes not the way you'd think . . . you'd start in Seattle, then down to L.A., then back up to Portland . . . they'd just run you ragged. So we'd gone on one of those long road trips and we probably took a red eye home, and we had a game that night. When we got back to Cleveland in the morning everybody else went home, and I went to one of our practice gyms at The Coliseum to work out. When I was done I went down the elevator, and when the door opened Bill was standing there. I said, 'See you in the locker room in four hours.' And he started me that night! We hadn't played very well of late and he figured, 'Let's change our lineup a little bit.' He never said anything to me. I'm sure that everyone in the locker room was going, 'What?' . . . including me! I had some other starts throughout my career but not many."

"Luke wasn't the fastest guy in the world," Thurmond said, "but he was a hard-working guy. He understood his role and was not a distraction if he didn't play. And when he played, he'd give you a hundred percent."

"He worked at it, no doubt about it," Joe Tait said.

Witte broke his left foot just prior to the start of the 1976–77 season and was on injured reserve for the entire year. "Back then," he said, "they weren't so quick to put the knife to feet so I didn't have surgery. In about January I'd gotten to the point where I could play again, but I'd lost about eight inches off my jump. And, considering how high I jumped, you could realize how bad that was! So I struggled through the rest of that season, practicing with the team but not dressing for games."

The Cavs released Witte after the season. He played in Europe that summer and the following season before calling it quits. Witte, along with his new bride Donita, to whom he is still married, returned to his former stomping grounds and bought a farm in Marlboro.

"We also owned a sporting goods store," he said. "I got into broadcasting, too, doing the color for college basketball games on SportsChannel Ohio. I also did Akron and Cleveland State games."

In the late 1980s, Witte finally acted on a calling that had nagged at him for years and would change the course of his life drastically—he, along with Donita, took after his old man and joined the ministry.

"Actually," he said, "that's the last thing I wanted to do. It's not that I'm an outstanding speaker or anything like that, I just love working with people and I think I'm fairly good at it."

Witte was the minister at a church in Charlotte, North Carolina, for more than a decade. These days, he works for Marketplace Chaplains USA as the Carolinas' division director, a position he has held for 11 years and which requires him to have a master affinity and be ordained. Witte and his leadership team oversee some 70 chaplains who work with people in stressful or challenging situations in their workplaces.

"We oversee about 2,000 employees and, with their families, about 28,000 people," he said, adding that he also recruits, trains, and develops the leadership teams.

Witte said the family turmoil he dealt with as a youngster helps him tremendously when counseling individuals and families. It has fueled his passion for helping people who are experiencing the same kinds of situations.

"I really enjoy helping people mend their problems before they get way beyond the point of no return," he said. "It's very fulfilling. It's amazing. I couldn't even begin to tell you all the different things we work with, the situations from the joys of a couple coming together and having a child to the horrors of suicide and everything in between. I can't think of anything I'd rather be doing."

Luke and Donita, who live in Charlotte, have three grown children— daughter Erin, who is the marketing director for a bicycle company in town; son Lyle, who lives in the mountains of North Carolina; and daughter Emily, who is an aspiring actress in New York City. Donita now works for Wells Fargo. She and Luke like to travel and go bicycling and kayaking. Luke's other hobbies are woodworking, home renovations, and . . . well . . . golf.

"If any of my friends heard me say that I play golf," he chuckled, "they'd fall on the floor laughing the way I play."

Witte also keeps tabs on the NBA—from a distance. "I keep up with it," he confessed, "just enough because everybody expects me to know what's going on. I do go to Hornets games once in a while."

In fact, when the Hornets, Charlotte's first NBA team, joined the league Witte was the team chaplain until they relocated to New Orleans, a period that included the tragic death of Hornets, and former Cavaliers, shooting guard Bobby Phills in an automobile accident.

After he moved to Marlboro when he was a boy, Witte lost touch with his father. They were estranged for several years. "In the mid-'90s," he said, "I found out he was living in Charleston, South Carolina. I just walked up to his door one day. It was a healing that I needed just to walk up to that door."

Asked about his relationship with Brewer, Witte paused before responding. "It's interesting," he said. "We'd actually known each other before the fight occurred. I'd always liked Jim. After the incident, the next time we saw each other was that summer at the Olympic tryout camp at the Air Force Academy in Colorado Springs. We actually sat down across the table from each other and kind of talked it through. We didn't get into real deep feelings, though."

When Witte and Brewer were rookies in 1973, Fitch used a tried-and-true method in hopes of mending any bad blood remaining between the two.

"The first day of camp," he said, "I put them together as roommates. The other players thought I was nuts. In fact, we had bets on how long the fight would last. I just decided to let them solve the problem together. I knew them both well enough to know that they were going to put the fight behind them." Fitch was right.

"We had an exhibition game down at St. John Arena in Columbus," Witte recalled. "Jim was walking into Columbus, and Columbus doesn't forget. The fans booed him during warmups. So every time Jim got his hands on the ball I just changed where I was in line, came up behind him, put my arm around him and said, 'Don't let it bother you. Forget the boos. Don't let it upset your game. You're in a different situation now.' And the boos stopped!"

That was quite an act of sportsmanship. It was also a sign of things to come for Witte in helping people with their problems.

Butch Beard

When Butch Beard arrived in Cleveland less than a month into the Cavaliers' 1971–72 season after receiving an "early-out" from the Army, he was in for quite a surprise. "They made me team captain!" he said.

The Cavs had lost 10 of their first 14 games after finishing just 15–67 in their first season the year before, so they probably felt that a guy like Alfred "Butch" Beard would be the logical choice for captain. It's true that Beard, whom the Cavs had acquired via the Expansion Draft the year before, had just one season of NBA experience under his belt—mainly as a backup in his rookie year of 1969–70 with the Atlanta Hawks—but the 6-foot-3, 185-pound point guard had made quite a name for himself prior to that. He was the 10th player chosen overall by the Hawks in the 1969 NBA Draft out of the University of Louisville. Four years earlier virtually every college in the nation recruited him. He and a guy by the name of Lew Alcindor were ranked by *Parade Magazine* as two of the top five high school players in the country.

"When I'd realized I was going to get out of the Army early," Beard recalled, "I had leave so I went to Cleveland's '71 training camp. So when I returned to the team after the season had started, I pretty much already knew what Coach [Bill] Fitch wanted to do. So it was pretty easy for me to make the adjustment."

The Cavaliers' new captain did not disappoint. He averaged 15.4 points and a team-leading 6.7 assists per game in '71–72 and made his only All-Star Game appearance. The Cavs still wound up 23–59 and in last place in the Central Division. Beard, though, has fond memories of that season.

"We were all trying to figure out how we could make our little niche and stay in the NBA," he said. "We had a coach who was only in his second season in the league. We were a young group of guys and we had a lot of fun."

Beard was born on May 4, 1947, in the small town of Hardinsburg, Kentucky. "I was about 10 years old when I got involved in sports," he said. "I started playing organized basketball in the seventh grade."

That year, Beard, who had three younger brothers, was one of the few seventh graders on his school's seventh/eighth-grade team, which won 30-plus games and was one of the better outfits in Kentucky. Four years later, as a junior, he led Breckinridge County High School to the state championship game. As a senior he led Breckinridge back to the title game and won it as he was named Kentucky Mr. Basketball. Beard played center for the Bearcats and had actually started on the high school team as an eighth grader, and before that, even played in a handful of high school junior varsity games when he was in the seventh grade!

"I'd played against older guys while I was coming up," he said, "so being the youngest out there didn't bother me."

Before he officially signed to attend Louisville, which is a little more than an hour's drive from Hardinsburg, Beard was home watching television one night when the phone rang. It was a gentleman by the name of John Wooden, UCLA's living-legend coach.

"I told Coach Wooden that I was going to stay close to home because my parents had gotten interested in watching me play," Beard said. "Later on that school year, Wooden coached me at an all-star game in Memphis, Tennessee. He came up to me and said, 'You know, you're the only kid I know who's turned me down.' I said, 'Well Coach, like I told you, it was just one of those things where I was going to try to stay as close to home as possible because of my family.'"

After starting at forward on Louisville's freshman team, Beard, still at forward, averaged a team-leading 20.5 points per game his sophomore year, helping the Cardinals to a 23–5 record and the Missouri Valley Conference Championship. However, in the NCAA Tournament the Cards, ranked second in the nation, were upset 83–81 by Southern Methodist in a Midwest Regional Semifinal. The next season, Beard, who was roommates with Wes Unseld, was switched to point guard, where he would remain for the rest of his career, including the NBA.

"I'd never played the guard positon," he said. "It was different, but it was the best thing that happened to me because if I'd have continued to play forward I don't know if I would've made it to the pros."

As a junior Beard averaged 16 points per game, but he and his teammates, again a top 10 club, fell 91–75 in the NCAA tourney to the Elvin Hayes–led Houston Cougars, again in a Midwest Regional Semifinal. In his senior year of 1968–69, Beard averaged a team-best 20.6 points per contest, but he and the Cardinals fell to Drake in the MVC Tournament.

During his rookie year with the Hawks, Beard eventually received substantial playing time when veteran Walt Hazzard needed some rest.

"That's when I started to figure out that I could play in the NBA," he said.

The Cavaliers traded Beard to Seattle prior to the 1972–73 season. After a year in the Pacific Northwest, he was dealt to Golden State, where he spent two seasons and was a key cog in the Warriors winning the NBA Championship in 1974–75, averaging 12.8 points and 4.2 assists per game. When he was traded back to the Cavs that offseason, Warriors guard Rick Barry, a future Hall of Famer, was dumbfounded.

"Rick said the biggest mistake Golden State ever made was getting rid of me," recalled Beard, who was confused himself. "I was surprised after we'd won the championship that they traded me, but, hey, I've been in many organizations. Sometimes they do strange things. I'll just leave it at that."

"In my opinion, Golden State failed to repeat in '75–76 because they didn't have Butch Beard," said Nate Thurmond, a teammate of Beard's for one season with the Warriors.

Beard spent little more than a month with the Cavs in 1975–76 before getting released on Thanksgiving night.

"Bill told me, 'You'll have no problem, you're gonna be picked up,'" he said. "I was about to go across the damned desk and beat his ass. I told him, 'How can I help one team win a championship and I can't play for a ball club that hasn't had a chance to win a championship?' Looking back, I think Bill thought he had a good enough team and didn't know how the hell to use all the players. We had five good guards—Jim Cleamons, Dick Snyder, Foots Walker, Austin Carr, and myself—and he just didn't know how to divvy up those minutes."

"Butch was a hell of a player," Fitch said. "This way, I gave him a chance to go somewhere else and get more playing time."

Beard proved Fitch prophetic as he was signed by New York in less than a week. He played for the Knicks through the 1978–79 season before retiring.

A Louisville Athletic Hall of Fame inductee, Beard had a stint as the color analyst for Knicks games on the MSG network during the 1980s. He then ventured into the coaching profession, reuniting with Fitch as one of his assistants with the New Jersey Nets before moving on to become the head coach at Howard University, where, in 1991–92, he led the Bison to the last of two appearances the school has made in the NCAA Tournament. Beard returned to the NBA as head coach of the Nets from 1994–96. He was also the head coach of Morgan State University.

Since retiring from coaching in 2006, Beard has worked with, and helped, New York City youth. He and his wife of eight years, Lisa, live in New York City. Beard has four grown children, three sons and a daughter, from a previous marriage, and three grandchildren. His second-oldest son, Cory, played for Dad at Howard.

Beard may not have had a Hall of Fame career in the pros, but he lasted nearly a decade and had his moments.

"Butch Beard," Mike Peticca said, "was certainly a quality NBA player."

Steve Patterson

When most college basketball fans think of the remarkable UCLA dynasty that brought 10 National Championships in 12 years to Bruin Land, the two players who usually come to mind first are Lew Alcindor (later Kareem Abdul-Jabbar) and Bill Walton. And why shouldn't they? After all, those two big men played pivotal parts in half of those 10 national titles—Alcindor in 1966–67, '67–68, and '68–69, and Walton in 1971–72 and '72–73. But what about the two seasons in between, 1969–70 and '70–71? UCLA won the National Championship in those two seasons, as well. The Bruins' starting center those two years? Future Cavalier Steve Patterson.

Patterson, a native of Riverside, California, where he was born on June 24, 1948, and a graduate of Santa Maria High School in Santa Maria, California, may not have hung up the extraordinary numbers in college that Alcindor and Walton did. He certainly held his own, though, and did his part in helping UCLA to those two national titles in 1970 and '71. After averaging an incredible 21.9 points and 20.2 rebounds per game on the Bruins' freshman team in 1966–67, then redshirting in '67–68 and backing up Alcindor in '68–69, Patterson netted 12.5 points and 10 rebounds per game as a junior, helping his team to a 28–2 record. He scored 17 points in the Bruins' 80–69 triumph over Jacksonville in the NCAA Championship Game. After the season, he was named the winner of the J. D. Morgan Memorial Award, presented by the Bruin Hoopsters for the outstanding "team player."

Because of his earlier redshirt season, Patterson was eligible for the 1970 NBA and ABA drafts. In fact, he was chosen by the Phoenix Suns of the NBA and the Texas Chaparrals of the ABA. Patterson passed up both opportunities to return to school for his senior year. He seemed to have made the right decision as he put up 12.9 points and 9.8 rebounds per contest, helping UCLA to a 29–1 record and the national title. In the championship game, he scored a career-high 29 points in the Bruins' 68–62 victory over Villanova.

The 6-foot-9, 225-pound Patterson was selected by the Cavaliers in the second round of the 1971 NBA Draft. Chronic knee problems limited him and caused him to play mainly as a backup center. He did have a productive season in 1973–74 when, as a starter for the better part of the schedule, he averaged 7.8 points, 8.1 rebounds, and 2.2 assists per game, all career highs. On February 16 that season he scored a career-high 22 points in a win over Portland, one of three games that year in which he tallied at least 20 points. Less than a year later, on January 19, 1975, Patterson topped his single-game points mark when he scored 23 against the Pistons.

Sheldon Ocker recalled that Patterson's first wife showed up at just about every home game while he was with the Cavs. But oddly, "She'd sit in the stands and never watch the game," he laughed. "She'd read a book."

Patterson was traded to the Chicago Bulls on Thanksgiving Day 1975. He finished out the '75–76 season in the Windy City and then played a year in Italy before retiring. He took a stab at coaching, first as the head coach at Santa Rosa Junior College from 1983–85 and then at Arizona State University from 1985–89. He was also the chairman of Phoenix's organizing committee for Super Bowl XXX and was the commissioner of the CBA in 1997. Patterson spent his last years organizing youth and community sports programs in Arizona, including as founder of the Grand Canyon State Games. He and his second wife Carlette ran Patterson Sports Ventures, which specialized in marketing for professional athletes, sports philanthropy, and sports ministries. Patterson was a gourmet cook, a history buff, and a wine connoisseur. He died of lung cancer on July 28, 2004.

Steve and Carlette have a daughter, and he had four children from his first marriage. A lifelong Christian, Patterson, who had started a ministry on campus while at UCLA, made faith the core of his post-NBA activities and is remembered at TheGoal.com, a website that had acted as his central organization for church-sports activities. In 2005, the Robert Wood Johnson Foundation established the Steve Patterson Award for Excellence in Sports Philanthropy because Patterson believed in, and practiced, the power of sports philanthropy to make a difference.

Patterson was also a likeable individual. "Steve was really an interesting guy," Joe Tait said. "I enjoyed getting to know him. He was one of my favorite people."

Eric Fernsten

Eric Fernsten is a survivor. Take his career in the NBA.

"I never started a game, even an exhibition one," he said. "But I played hard in practice and took it upon myself to always be ready to come off the bench if needed."

One of those times was during Game 7 of the Eastern Conference Finals on May 3, 1981, in the hallowed Boston Garden. A member of the Cavaliers five years earlier, Fernsten was a backup center for the Celtics, who were opposing their chief rival in the Atlantic Division, the Philadelphia 76ers, the team that had beaten Boston in the same round the year before.

"Ten seconds before halftime, [head coach] Bill [Fitch] threw me in there to take a foul," Fernsten recalled. "I ran up to Julius Erving, reached for the ball and caught his arm for the foul with two seconds left. Then they lobbed the ball toward the basket, 'Max' [Cedric Maxwell] knocked it down, toward me, I saved it from going out of bounds and threw it to Robert Parish as time ran out. So they didn't get a shot off. After the game [which the Celtics won 91–90] in the locker room I couldn't even dress because Max's locker, which was next to mine, was surrounded by media people. So I'm in the middle of the locker room dressing and here comes Julius Erving. He looks around, he walks right up to me and goes, 'Great foul' and shakes my hand. There was a picture of it in the *Boston Globe* the next day. It was amazing!"

Fernsten was born on November 1, 1953, in Oakland, California. He actively participated in sports until the summer before middle school when he took on a paper route, a job he held until two weeks before he entered Skyline High School. That's when he was bitten by the basketball "bug." It's also when his "survival skills" surfaced.

"As a sophomore I made the JV team on pure attitude," he said. "I worked hard the next summer and by my junior year I was coming off the bench on the varsity team."

By the time he was a senior, Fernsten was starting and earned All-League honors. Of the dozen or so full scholarships he was offered, he chose to play for the University of San Francisco. The Dons' winning tradition and an encouraging phone call from San Francisco alum, and future NBA Hall of Famer, Bill Russell greased the wheels. After starting at center, where he would remain for most of the rest of his basketball career, on the freshman team in 1971–72, as a sophomore Fernsten averaged eight points and nine rebounds per game, helping San Fran to a 23–5 record and the West Coast Conference title. Included was a 20-rebound performance against Loyola Marymount.

Twice that season Fernsten and the Dons went up against John Wooden's famed UCLA Bruins, who were in the midst of legendary runs of 88 straight wins and 10 NCAA titles in 12 years. The first meeting was on January 19 at the home of the Bruins, Pauley Pavilion. UCLA won 92–64.

"Going up against Bill Walton and that gang was a pretty big baptism for me," Fernsten said. "They were really flying high on us. UCLA had won 57 games in a row and was nearing the record of 60 by, coincidentally, San Francisco, when Russell was there for most of them."

Fernsten and his teammates got another shot at the Bruins some two months later in the NCAA Tournament. The Dons lost the rematch 54–39 in the West Regional Final after having disposed of Long Beach State 77–67 in a regional semifinal. The next year, Fernsten averaged 9.3 points and 10 rebounds per game as San Francisco repeated as WCC champs and finished 19–9. It beat New Mexico 64–61 in a West Regional Semifinal but fell to—who else?—UCLA in the Regional Final 83–60. As a senior, Fernsten was able to muster 7.9 points and 9.2 boards per contest, helping the Dons to a 19–7 record. This was after he spent the entire summer in bed recovering from mononucleosis. At this point, Fernsten had no clue that he had even a remote shot of playing in the NBA.

"I didn't even expect to be drafted," he said, "until after our last game my senior year at Pepperdine." That's when soon-to-be Pepperdine star, and future NBA Hall of Famer, Dennis Johnson approached Fernsten. "He said, 'Fernsten, good luck in the pros,'" Eric recalled. "I said, 'What?' I had no idea I was anywhere near pro material."

A business administration major, Fernsten was chosen by the Cavaliers in the fourth round of the 1975 NBA Draft. He was also selected by the Kentucky Colonels in the ABA Draft.

"When I left for Cleveland," he said, "it was really the first time I'd been away from home. It was a whirlwind adjustment trying to figure out what was going on around me."

Just as he would later that decade in Boston, the 6-foot-9, 205-pound Fernsten, who made the 1975–76 Cavs as a backup center, focused on being ready if his name was called. "I'd try to stay in shape," he said, "by running outside rain or shine when we were on the road."

Fernsten, however, lasted little more than a month in the wine and gold. Fitch traded him to Chicago, where he was a member of the Bulls for the rest of '75–76 and in '76–77 before being released. He played two seasons in Italy before reuniting with Fitch in Boston, where, in addition to center, he backed up at power forward and netted three of his four career-best 11-point games in his first season there, 1979–80.

"I learned everything pretty much from the bench," Fernsten said. "Just like always, I watched the games closely so I could plug in wherever they needed me to play. Because most of my bench time was spent next to Coach Fitch, I began to anticipate substitutions, timeouts, and how to counter the opponent's strategy. Bill was always so prepared and quick on his feet to adjust to game situations. Each game was a remarkable learning experience for me."

"Fans rarely got to see Eric play," Fitch said, "until a game was decided one way or the other. But we won a couple ball games when he was with

Eric Fernsten defends against the Pistons in exhibition action, October 1975. (The Cleveland Press Collection, Michael Schwartz Library, Cleveland State University)

me in Boston when he went in because of foul trouble or injuries. Eric was also a tremendous practice player. Many times, he'd play better in practice than the guy he was imitating! He was a great team player and never complained about lack of minutes."

"Many of my ex-teammates," Fernsten said, "have acknowledged my importance in their books and interviews over the years, and I've appreciated that greatly."

Fernsten spent three years in Beantown—including an NBA Championship in 1981—before retiring and venturing into the world of finance, working for a major Wall Street company for a year. He returned to the game he loved and spent his final NBA season of 1983–84 as a backup power forward for the New York Knicks. Brief stints in the CBA and United States Basketball League followed before he hung up the sneakers for good.

Not too long ago, Fernsten came across a behind-the-scenes television special about Erving, or "Dr. J."

"It was interesting," he said. "After Philadelphia lost to Portland in the 1977 Finals, all the Sixers players were really mad. Julius said to them, 'Let's go into Portland's locker room and congratulate them.' And the guys were like, 'I want to go in there and fight them! I hate those guys!' And Julius said, 'No-o-o-o, we'll congratulate them.' Erving's teammates refused to go, so by himself Julius went into the Portland locker room to offer his congratulations.

"Now I know why four years later Julius came into the Celtics' locker room to shake my hand. The next year, in '82, we had another Conference Finals seventh game with the Sixers in Boston, and they beat us. And I didn't even know that I should've gone back and said to Julius, 'Beat L.A.!' [since the Lakers would be Philly's opponent in the Finals]. At the time, I didn't know why he'd come up to me the year before. But that's what Julius did when he lost. He congratulated the victors. At that time, you never really talked with your opponents, mingled, because they were your opponents! But now, in the NBA, and in the NFL, too, after games opposing players are slapping hands with, and hugging, one another. I think that's really cool. They respect, and they know about, each other."

These days, Fernsten is semi-retired and lives with his family in Northern California. He does some consulting, including scouting for an ex-teammate who is the head coach of a women's Division I college team. He also has recently joined the National Basketball Retired Players Association.

"I've been out of touch with everybody. I walked away from it almost completely," he said. "I'm trying to reach out to some of the guys I used to compete with."

Although he feels blessed to have played in the NBA, Fernsten does have one regret—that he began playing basketball later than most boys.

"I was always playing catch-up to everyone around me," he said. "I may have had the physical tools to play, but I was always in doubt as to how good I was."

Fernsten is what one would call a deep thinker. He's a witty individual, so much so that he likes to tell people that his uniform number with the Bulls—23—is retired.

"Eric was an interesting fellow," Joe Tait said. "I enjoyed talking to him."

Fernsten is putting his creative mind to use, as he is in the process of writing several screenplays.

"One's about my career in the NBA," he said. "I know it's a long shot, but maybe one day it'll make it to the big screen."

Why not? After all, Fernsten was a long shot to make it to the NBA. But he did.

Postscript

The 1975–76 Cleveland Cavaliers were unique. Not only did they enjoy success on the basketball court, they also enjoyed one another's company off it. There were no egos, no animosities, no jealousies. Their relationships off the court helped their chemistry on it.

"We spent a lot of time at each other's homes, we socialized and relaxed together," said Jim Cleamons. "And it was a wonderful culmination of those friendships, and of those of us who'd endured all the losing and the belittling of being a Cavalier, that resulted in the comeuppance of becoming a franchise that was worthy of the adulation it received."

"That '75–76 team was a special group," Nate Thurmond said. "It was just incredible to share the success we had with those guys who you really enjoyed playing with and being around off the court. We played hard, practiced hard, and our success was just the fruits of our labor."

Said Rowland Garrett, "It's unusual to find 12 guys who get along so well. That Cavs team was the greatest group of guys I ever had the pleasure of playing with. It was like a family."

The one thing that stands out in Bill Fitch's mind is that, all these years later, the team members, including himself, still convene for reunions and golf outings.

"That also includes the ball boys!" he said. "Those guys had—and still have—a genuine love and respect for one another. I love them all. They're like adopted sons, the sons I never had. And our fans, because of the way those guys played, they were . . . visitors would come in and when they'd leave they'd say, 'You've got the damnedest fans!'"

"That whole 1975–76 season was like a fairy tale," Charlie Strasser said.

"It really was," said Jim Chones. "Forty years later people still talk about it."

Index